Language for Study

LEVEL 3

Alistair McNair   Fred Gooch

Series editor: Ian Smallwood

CAMBRIDGE
UNIVERSITY PRESS
www.cambridge.org

CAMBRIDGE UNIVERSITY PRESS
Cambridge, New York, Melbourne, Madrid, Cape Town,
Singapore, São Paulo, Delhi, Mexico City

Cambridge University Press
The Edinburgh Building, Cambridge CB2 8RU, UK

www.cambridge.org
Information on this title: www.cambridge.org/9781107681101

First published 2013

Printed and bound in the United Kingdom by the MPG Books Group

A catalogue record for this publication is available from the British Library

ISBN 978-1-107-68110-1 Paperback

Acknowledgements
The authors and publishers acknowledge the following
sources of copyright material and are grateful for the
permissions granted. While every effort has been made,
it has not always been possible to identify the sources of
all the material used, or to trace all copyright holders.
If any omissions are brought to our notice, we will be
happy to include the appropriate acknowledgements
on reprinting.

Author acknowledgements
The authoring team would like to thank Clare Sheridan,
Nik White, Jo Garbutt, Ian Morrison and the editorial
team at Cambridge for their constant help and support
throughout the whole project. We also offer our grateful
acknowledgement to Sarah Clark and Neil McSweeney
for their advice and invaluable contributions to the
manuscripts. Finally, we would like to thank all ELT
and academic skills staff and students across Kaplan
International Colleges for their assistance in trialling
the materials during development and for their valuable
feedback and suggestions.

Publisher acknowledgements
The Guardian for the text on p.99 adapted from
'Why I am against biometric ID cards' by Charles Arthur,
29 February 2008. Copyright Guardian News & Media
Ltd 2010; The Guardian for Text D on p.103 adapted from
'Was it right to scrap the ContactPoint child database?'
by Penny Nicholls, 13 August 2010. Copyright Guardian
News & Media Ltd 2010.

Photo ackowledgements
p.4 t-b ©ktsimage/istockphotos.com, ©andrey
Pavlov/istock, ©Image_Source/istockphoto.com,
©mattjeacockistock; p.6 © ktsimage/istockphotos.
com; p.28©Art Directors & TRIP / Alamy; p.47 ©andrey
Pavlov/istock; p48 ©appleuzr/istockphoto.com; p.57
©Alex Segre / Alamy; p86 ©Image_Source/istockphoto.
com; p.123 ©MiRafoto.com / Alamy; p.130 ©Kevin Foy /
Alamy; p.134 ©mattjeacockistock; p.152 ©Peter D Noyce
/ Alamy; p.172 ©Lou Linwei / Alamy

Design and illustrations by Hart McLeod, Cambridge

Language for Study Contents

Map of the book

Understanding

	Speaking Part A	Writing Part B
1 An electronic world	Identifying features of fluent speech Understanding how pauses, intonation and stress influence listeners	Identifying appropriate academic style Referring to different authors' ideas Identifying persuasive language
► LESSON TASK	**Preparing and presenting a short, persuasive talk**	**Recognizing persuasion in texts**
2 New frontiers	Recognizing and using stressed and unstressed syllables in tone units Identifying lead-in and question structures	Identifying signposting for written arguments and counter-arguments Identifying assumptions Identifying and using word-order inversion
► LESSON TASK	**Forming questions after listening**	**Evaluating the basis of an argument**
3 The individual in society	Identifying the language of speculation Identifying the language of past speculation Identifying consonants and intrusive sounds	Understanding the way claims are framed Evaluating claims in context
► LESSON TASK	**Speculating on a topic**	**Identifying and assessing claims**
4 Choices	Identifying and understanding repetition Identifying and understanding reformulation Identifying stance markers	Identifying emphasis in academic texts Identifying and understanding analogy in academic texts
► LESSON TASK	**Identifying a speaker's stance on a topic**	**Reading to recognize emphasis in texts**
	Appendices	

Investigating

Reporting

Part C	Speaking Part D	Writing Part E
Identifying the grammatical structure of reporting verbs Identifying reporting verb collocations	Identifying rise and fall tones for checking and adding new information Identifying and using tones for authority and finishing a topic	Identifying general–specific structure in introductions Identifying linking words used in introductions Writing and paraphrasing definitions using academic nouns
Reporting other people's ideas	**Identifying phrases used in a group presentation**	**Organizing introductions**
Identifying and using hedging devices Identifying vocabulary and grammar used in stating premises	Referring to graphics and visual data Referring to other sources in a presentation (1)	Using *it* and *this* to link between sentences Using *it* phrases to convey opinion
Hedging an argument	**Referring to other sources in a presentation (2)**	**Identifying cohesion in texts**
Reconstructing information from notes Writing when synthesizing information from two or more sources	Summarizing key aspects of research in a presentation Presenting an oral argument with alternative viewpoints	Identifying and using substitution and ellipsis Identifying and using different ways of paraphrasing
Using synthesis in writing	**Including alternative views in a presentation**	**Paraphrasing a text**
Identifying common errors in formality levels of academic emails Understanding appropriate features of emails in different situations Identifying formal and informal language in written communication	Concluding an oral presentation Speculating about research results in conclusions	Developing language for writing conclusions Referring to previous sections of an academic text in the conclusion Expressing importance, desirability and necessity
Writing a formal email	**Presenting results of research**	**Writing a conclusion**

Unit 1 An electronic world

Unit overview

Part	This part will help you to ...	By improving your ability to ...
A	**Listen more effectively in lectures**	• identify features of fluent speech • understand how pauses, intonation and stress influence listeners.
B	**Become familiar with different types of written text**	• identify appropriate academic style • refer to different authors' ideas • identify persuasive language.
C	**Develop critical-thinking skills**	• identify the grammatical structure of reporting verbs • identify reporting verb collocations.
D	**Prepare effective oral presentations**	• identify rise and fall tones for checking and adding new information • identify and use tones for authority and finishing a topic.
E	**Develop essay-writing skills**	• identify general–specific structure in introductions • identify linking words used in introductions • write and paraphrase definitions using academic nouns.

Understanding spoken information

By the end of Part A you will be able to:

- identify features of fluent speech
- understand how pauses, intonation and stress influence listeners.

1 Identifying features of fluent speech

1a Work in pairs. What is the difference between academic disciplines which are:

1 so-called 'hard' (paradigmatic) or 'soft' (non-paradigmatic)?

2 pure or applied?

3 life or non-life?

1b Complete the sentences below with the phrases in the box. Then check your answers with a partner.

economics or sociology　　　physics or chemistry

1 If you are listening to a lecture in ＿＿＿＿＿＿＿ , you will be expected to think critically about what you hear.

2 If you are listening to a lecture in ＿＿＿＿＿＿＿ , you will be expected to know and understand all the basic concepts and agreed facts of the subject before you hear the lecture.

When listening to a lecture, you need to be aware that fluent speech is characterized by certain key features which can affect the way a word is pronounced in context.

In fluent speech:

1 the final consonant of a word which ends with two (or more) consonant sounds (e.g. /s/ and /t/ in *most*) is not pronounced when it comes before a word which begins with a consonant (e.g. *probable*)

2 unstressed vowels (/ə/) in words of more than one syllable are often not pronounced, especially when they come before a /r/, /l/ or /n/ sound (e.g. *charact/ə/ristic*)

3 an extra consonant sound – /w/, /j/ or /r/ – is pronounced when a word that ends in a vowel sound (e.g. *to*) comes before a word starting with a vowel (*an*)

4 the final consonant sound at the end of a word (e.g. *look*) links to the following word if it begins with a vowel sound (e.g. *at*). Note that it is the sound at the end of the word that is important, so beware of silent vowels (e.g. *excessive electricity*).

1c Work in pairs. Read the introduction to a lecture on p.8, looking carefully at the bold words and phrases. Then identify at least one example of each of the four features of fluent speech described above. Some highlighted parts may demonstrate more than one feature.

Today we're going to **take a look at** the characteristic **differences** between **various academic** disciplines. **The most familiar** distinction, perhaps, **for a lot of** people, is the **division of academic** subjects into so-called 'hard' and 'soft' categories, with the 'hard' subjects being the physical sciences, mainly, and the **'soft' subjects** the humanities and social sciences. But what **does it** really mean when we say **that a subject is** hard or soft? **Does it have any implications** for the ways that students learn? The hard–**soft distinction** comes from research done in the 1970s by the psychologist Anthony Biglan. He **studied a number of different academic disciplines** and proposed that they could be **divided along three axes**: firstly, 'hard' or 'soft'; secondly, 'pure' or 'applied'. There's **also a** third and final distinction into 'life' or 'non-life'.

1.1

1d Listen and check your answers.

1e Work in pairs. Decide how these short phrases would be pronounced in fluent speech.

1 It's a simple enough distinction …

2 This is hopefully …

3 But let's look more closely at …

4 To an extent, …

5 … in the course of …

6 This explains to some extent why …

7 … on the other hand …

8 There's a strong consensus about the way …

9 It's particularly important …

10 So we can see that there are clear differences between …

1.2

1f Listen and check your answers. Then practise saying the phrases, using the features of fluent speech you have identified.

2 Understanding how pauses, intonation and stress influence listeners

In lectures, especially in 'soft' (non-paradigmatic) subjects, the speaker is often trying to persuade the audience to accept the argument that they are presenting. The speaker can strengthen their argument through their choice of:

1 the language used

2 references to supporting information or material

3 pauses, intonation and stress used.

In this section, the focus will be on understanding the third feature only.

2a Work in pairs. Read the extract below from a lecture on the 'digital divide' and identify the lecturer's main argument.

Now, several studies, such as work by Chris Kelvin in 2003 and Paul De Soto's 2007 article *The Divided World*, have identified the digital divide as being, basically, a problem of technology. In essence, they claim that the internet digital divide is similar to what was seen with TV and other emergent, or new, technologies. Such technologies are first of all adopted in certain leading-edge centres and then, slowly, they spread themselves over time until they become nearly universal.

I take an opposite view to Kelvin and De Soto. I would claim that there is a more fundamental problem with the digital divide. That the digital divide is a deeper social and economic issue, which means that some societies – such as those in the developing world – or communities within a society – such as poorer and more marginal groups in industrialized nations – are incapable of getting access to the Internet. And that this lack of internet access exacerbates existing economic and educational problems.

2b Think about how a lecturer can use pauses, intonation and stress to help persuade a listener to accept the argument. First, make notes on how each feature might be used to persuade. Then compare your ideas with a partner.

Notes

Feature	How each feature might be used to support an argument	How the features are used by this lecturer
Pauses		
Intonation		
Stress		

1.3

2c Now read and listen to the first paragraph of the lecture extract in 2a. While you listen, mark:

- pauses with a slash (/) between words
- intonation with a rise (↗) or fall (↘) arrow above phrases
- words with very prominent stress with a circle (○) over the word.

2d Use your annotated script in 2a to make notes in the right-hand column of the table in 2b.

2e Work in pairs. Use your notes to say how the choice of pauses, intonation and stress can influence a listener. Then discuss where you think the speaker might use pauses and stress in the second paragraph in 2a, and where you might expect the intonation to rise and fall. Remember, there is no 'correct' answer to this question.

1.4

2f Listen to the second part of the lecture extract. Then discuss whether or not the lecturer used the pauses, intonation and stress in the way you expected.

> Intonation is also important because it tells us what kind of message we are receiving. Intonation can be used by a speaker to show that they are:
> • giving new information
> • asking a question
> • checking
> • expressing authority
> • signalling the end of an idea.

2g Look at these sentences and identify which of the functions in the box above match each one.

1 'There are two very important factors: technology and cost.'

2 'Finally, we can conclude that the divide is permanent.'

3 'Sorry, professor. Did you say "technology" and "cost"?'

4 'However, the Internet is clearly very useful.'

5 'Could you explain the difference again, please?'

> Short sentences may rise or fall, but longer sentences are very likely to have several changes in intonation. This, combined with stress, gives spoken English its characteristic sound.

1.5

2h Listen to a sentence from the first paragraph of the extract in 2a, which has been divided into small sections. In each section, decide whether the word in bold has a rise (↗) or fall (↘) tone.

1 _____ In **essence**,

2 _____ they **claim** that

3 _____ the internet **digital** divide

4 _____ is **similar** to what was seen

5 _____ with **TV**

6 _____ and **other** emergent,

7 _____ or **new**,

8 _____ **technologies**.

3 Preparing and presenting a short, persuasive talk

3a You are going to listen to an extract from a lecture about the Internet and the use of energy. Before you listen, discuss whether you think these statements are true (T) or false (F). Give reasons for your answers.

	True (T)	False (F)
1 Increasing numbers of people watch TV or listen to the radio online.		
2 It is more energy efficient to watch TV on the Internet than on a normal, dedicated TV set.		
3 It is more energy efficient to listen to radio on the Internet than on a normal, dedicated radio.		
4 Internet-associated energy use has decreased over the past few years.		

1.6

3b Listen and check your ideas against the speaker's position.

3c Read the lecture extract below and identify:

1 the speaker's main argument

2 any words and phrases used to persuade the listener

3 references to supporting information or material to support the argument.

> Now some of these things, like TV and radio, were previously delivered to the home using other devices, but since 2007 there has been an enormous rise in the number of people using the Internet to watch TV shows that they could have watched on their home TV set, or likewise listening to radio shows online rather than switching on a dedicated home radio. The evidence is clear that using the Internet for this kind of content actually requires more power consumption than if the user were to use a regular TV or radio. Looking at the figures for TV, we see here that average power consumption for a desktop computer is between 100 and 150 watts, with a laptop being rather less than half of that. By contrast, TVs stand at 74 watts.

3d Imagine you are preparing to give this lecture. Think about where you could use pauses, which words you might stress and how you could use intonation to influence the listeners. Read the extract again and mark:

- pauses you want to make with a slash (/) between words
- your choice of intonation with a rise (↗) or fall (↘) tone appropriate to the type of message you want to express
- words you want to stress most prominently with a circle (○) over the word.

3e Work in pairs. Take turns to listen to each other reading the text in 3c. When it is your turn to listen, mark the pauses, intonation and prominent stress that your partner uses on the extract in **Appendix 1**.

3f Take turns to compare the annotations you made on the lecture extract in 3d with the notes your partner made in **Appendix 1**. How similar or different are the two sets of notes? Discuss why you think this might be.

3g Choose *one* of the topics below (1–4), then prepare and deliver a one- or two-minute talk. Write out your script first, using words / phrases and references to material which you think will help you to influence your listeners. Then annotate your script, thinking about how you can use pauses, intonation and stress most effectively to persuade your audience to support your position.

1 Listening to the radio is more interesting than watching television.

2 Texting is better than phoning.

3 Mobile phones are bad for your health.

4 Shopping online is more fun than going to the shops.

3h Work in pairs to practise your presentation. When it is your turn to listen, make notes on your partner's performance using this table. Then use your notes to give feedback.

Was your partner ...	Yes	No	Example phrase
speaking too fast?			
speaking too slowly?			
pausing?			
stressing words?			
using rise tones?			
using fall tones?			

3i Work in groups of four or five. Present the talk you prepared in 3g and practised in 3h to the group, thinking about the feedback you received to improve your delivery.

4 Review and extension

1.7

4a Listen to a lecturer trying to persuade his students to use the university Virtual Learning Environment (VLE). What reasons does the lecturer give?

> In this task, the focus is on the speaker's use of language rather than the stress and intonation of their speech. The lecturer is not presenting an argument, but is making a strong recommendation. However, he still uses similar persuasive techniques to the ones that you have studied in *Skills for Study Level 3* and also in Part A of this unit.

4b Listen again and complete the extract. Each gap contains two or three words only. Then check your answers with a partner.

> You **1)** _____ the VLE, you know. There are lots of activities on it which will supplement your time in class. You only **2)** _____ hour's seminar a week, and I can't possibly answer all your emails at once. On the VLE, there are materials, exercises and so on, and you can chat with your classmates if you have any questions. If you **3)** _____ , you'll miss out. It's probably fair to say that those students who use it the most do tend to produce better work.
>
> I **4)** _____ time-consuming, and there are not enough computers, but it's **5)** _____ you do have all day at your disposal.

4c Identify examples of the four features of fluent speech you studied in this unit in each of these sentences.

1 The past couple of years or so have seen increasing claims that the kind of content that people view on the Internet can cause excessive electricity consumption.

2 Clearly, with an increase in the number of users, there is also an increase in the energy which they consume while using the Net.

3 It is, in fact, almost certain that using the Internet to view this kind of content is more energy efficient than using a separate, dedicated machine, and that this efficiency will continue to improve.

1.8

4d Now listen to the sentences and check your ideas.

Understanding written information

By the end of Part B you will be able to:

- identify appropriate academic style
- refer to different authors' ideas
- identify persuasive language.

1 Identifying appropriate academic style

1a Read the extracts from three different types of academic text (A–C) and answer these questions.

    1 What academic discipline(s) do you think each text might belong to?

    2 What text type do you think each extract is? Choose from this list.

            dissertation   essay   report   research article   textbook

    3 Which part of the text do you think each extract comes from? Choose from this list.

            abstract   introduction   main body   conclusion

A The rapid spread of the Internet in the last years of the 20th century saw a renewal of the fear, in some quarters, that it would mean a creeping spread of westernization and the further erosion of local cultures around the world.

B Other reasons for differing results include very specific corpora, such as Sittig (2003), who investigated emails sent by patients to GPs (general practitioners). Gimenez (2000), on the other hand, found his email sample (consisting of 63 emails) to be informal and personalized (ibid, p.242).

C Recent years have seen increasing claims that the kind of content that people view on the Internet can cause excessive electricity consumption. This paper will compare internet use for viewing video and TV with the electricity demand from viewing the same type of content on a dedicated set, and investigate claims of an internet 'electricity drain'.

1b Work in pairs. Two of the three extracts in 1a include the use of persuasive language. Which of these language features can you find which help make the writing more persuasive?

- adjectives
- comparisons
- idioms
- metaphors
- personalization
- quotations

1c You will be looking more closely at the language of persuasion in Part B Section 3. First, make notes in the box below on these questions.

1 Which of the language features in 1b do you think are most effective for persuasion in academic writing?

2 Which features do you know (or do you think) are most common in academic writing in your chosen field?

Notes

1d Discuss your ideas in small groups.

2 Referring to different authors' ideas

> Writers can make their argument more persuasive by including references to the research they have done and by identifying authors who support their argument. However, it is important to be able to differentiate between the different authors' ideas when referring to them in an essay.

2a Work in pairs. Read the two extracts below from an essay on hard and soft academic subjects. Then discuss these questions with your partner.

1 What is the writer's opinion of Becher and Newman's work?

2 What language does the writer use to show her opinion?

3 In each sentence, whose ideas are you reading? The writer's, or Becher and Newman's?

4 In each sentence, whose words are you reading? The writer's, or Becher and Newman's?

A The past two decades have seen an increasing awareness of the subtleties and diversity of expression in different fields of study. Seminal studies such as Becher (1989) have clearly demonstrated the way different academic disciplines build, shape and express meaning.

B Newman (2001) notes that monographs are used more frequently (and earlier for undergraduate students) in the 'soft' disciplines.

2b Read this extract from a published essay and the paraphrase of the extract in a student's essay assignment. Then answer the questions below.

> The United States owes its powerful economic status in part to the creation of the Federal Reserve System in 1913, and particularly to the Bretton Woods agreement after World War II, which saw the United States given a central role in the world economy, leading to its ascendancy as the global reserve currency.

Source: Cohen, C. (2010). The decline of US economic power? *The Weekly*, p.42

> America owes its dominant economy to the formation in 1913 of the Federal Reserve System (Cohen, 2010, p.42).

1 Does the paraphrase express Cohen's ideas or the student's?

2 Are the words repeated from Cohen or completely paraphrased by the student?

3 Do you think the student agrees or disagrees with Cohen?

2c Work in pairs. Read extracts from six other students who were given the same assignment, and who have also decided to refer to Cohen in their essays. For each extract, answer questions 1–3 from 2b.

> 1 'The United States owes its powerful economic status ...' (Cohen, 2010).

> 2 Cohen (2010) argues that the United States has a strong economic position because of ...

> 3 Cohen (2010) claims that the US is in a strong economic position due to ...

> 4 Cohen (2010) points out that 'The United States owes its powerful economic status ...'

> 5 As Cohen (2010) points out, 'The United States owes its powerful economic status ...'

> 6 The United States owes its powerful economic status ...

2d Read this extract from a text on video-conferencing technology, which refers to two different authors: Siebert and Morena. Then underline all the phrases in the extract which show the writers' opinions of Siebert and Morena.

> It is necessary to reach a meaningful definition of high and low status within the workforce. Siebert's (1997, p.203) classic distinction draws the line between high and low status staff, depending on executive decision-making privilege. Morena (2006), however, has offered a subtle alternative in which the status distinction is derived from staff intuitions. Therefore, the working definition of what it is to be a 'high' status staff member is taken from the opinions of the staff in the workplace being studied.
>
> Siebert's definition has the advantage of being the commonly accepted one, having been used in a number of key studies into status effects. However, it suffers in our view from the necessity of further defining which decisions are 'executive'; many lower ranking staff enjoy decision-making powers but would not be recognized as 'high status' by their peers. In this regard, Moreno's definition seems to offer a clearer view of the reality of status distinctions within any given organization.
>
> In the present study, we have chosen to follow Morena's definition. 'High-status' staff are therefore defined as being those within the organization who the staff members themselves perceive as holding executive decision-making privileges.

2e Use the phrases you underlined in 2d to complete these notes.

Notes		
Reference	More positive phrases	More negative phrases
Siebert (1997)	classic distinction	
Morena (2006)		

2f You are going to write three different paraphrases of a reference. First, read the text below from Wu (2009). Then use the space which follows to write a paraphrase which:

a is more positive and agrees with Wu

b is more negative and disagrees with Wu

c expresses neither agreement nor disagreement with Wu.

> The rapid spread of the Internet in the last years of the 20th century saw a renewal of the fear, in some quarters, that it would mean a creeping spread of westernization and the further erosion of local cultures around the world.

Source: Wu, Z. (2009). Communications technology and culture. *The Weekly*, p.101.

Paraphrases
a
b
c

3 Identifying persuasive language

3a Look at this extract. Which device does the writer use in the second sentence to persuade the reader of their opinion?

> The proposed police computer database would go much further than any previous legislation has allowed. It would be the same as allowing a government inspector to follow you everywhere you went.

3b Work in pairs. Think of other devices that the writer can use to persuade a reader to accept their ideas.

3c Read this introduction to an essay on 'hard' and 'soft' subjects at university and underline any persuasive phrases. Then compare your answers with a partner.

Disciplinary differences in higher education

The past two decades have seen an increasing awareness of the subtleties and diversity of expression in different fields of study. Seminal studies such as Becher (1989) have clearly demonstrated the way different academic disciplines build, shape and express meaning. The traditional division of fields of study into hard and soft disciplines is reflected in the types of media through which written information is presented to students or, more precisely, the types of media which students are expected to look to for knowledge. The following paper will briefly outline some of the key distinctions between written text types used in differing categories of discipline following Biglan's (1973) framework, before making some tentative recommendations for use at an institutional level.

3d Read the descriptions of persuasive devices used in writing in the left-hand column of this table. Which, if any, of the devices did you find in the text in 3c? Add them to the right-hand column.

Persuasive device	Example(s) in the text
Presenting evidence and examples to support the author's claim.	
Emphasizing consensus with other authors.	
Using (large) numbers to demonstrate weight of evidence.	
Using emotive vocabulary to convince the reader that something is true when, in fact, it may only be a theory.	
Appealing to common sense and reason.	
Extending easily acceptable propositions by applying to less acceptable claims.	
Using analogy to show similarities between ideas.	

3e   Read these eight extracts. Underline all the examples of persuasive language you can find, then add them to the table in 3d.

1 This would tend to support the view that email is perceived as being somewhat like a letter, with the expectation of proper politeness formalities.

2 Denman's study was particularly broad, gathering results from a total of 9,000 workers in 200 US businesses, which demonstrated an overwhelming feeling among US office staff that email was a primary workplace stressor.

3 **Email is, of course, absolutely not an instantaneous form of communication, in the way that a phone conversation is.**

4 Whereas Tycho (1997) considered only twelve cases, the current paper is based on findings from 143 interviews conducted with institute staff during the 1993–1997 period.

5 Other studies in Europe have echoed the results of Denman's work, and it now seems irrefutable that email, despite its many benefits, is also a cause of significant workplace stress, rather than a mere inconvenience.

6 The evidence overwhelmingly indicates that email is a significant cause, perhaps the primary cause, of modern workplace stress. It is important that the evident benefits of email do not cause us to overlook this fact, or minimize its impact on workplace well-being, job satisfaction, and the dreadful consequences of stress-related illness.

7 Numerous studies (Bergson, 1988; Calderon & Watts, 1991; Baranwal, 2001, 2003a, 2003b) have demonstrated the link between internet dependency and lower attention span.

8 We sincerely hope that this paper will be understood for what it is: a call to arms. It is vital that government and the private sector cooperate to ensure that those who suffer in economically deprived areas of our own cities are offered the same chances for success and happiness as their more fortunate peers.

> **LESSON TASK**   **4   Recognizing persuasion in texts**

4a   Work in pairs. Discuss what impact you think the list of things on p.20 has had on how people:
- interact socially
- learn
- think.

computer games   email   instant messaging service

mobile phones   the Internet   video-conferencing software / hardware

4b Work in two groups. Each group will read the first part of a different journal article in **Appendix 2**. One group should read Text A (*The next generation of educational engagement*) and the other should read Text B (*Mobile technologies: prospects for their use in learning in informal science settings*). First, find and underline all the persuasive phrases in your text and then make a note of them in the Notes box below. Then summarize the key points the text is trying to make.

Notes
Persuasive devices used:
Summary of key points:

4c Now work with a student from the other group and give an oral summary of your text using the notes. Then describe the persuasive devices you have recorded.

4d Read the other text. Then discuss with your partner which of the phrases you underlined in 4b are the most persuasive, and which the least. Why?

5 Review and extension

5a Read the four extracts on p.21 (A–D) from an article on the decline of US economic power written by Lawson & Partridge, 2010. Then, for each extract, write a paraphrase in the Notes box which follows. When you paraphrase, show the reader whether you agree or disagree with Lawson and Partridge. An example has been done for you.

> However, recent events within US financial markets, combined with the emergence of new economic powers in the last decade, have led to a gradual erosion of US economic dominance.

Notes
As Lawson and Partridge (2010) suggest, there has been a slow reduction in the economic dominance of the USA.

A The US has enjoyed unparalleled advantages, which have added to its already considerable economic might.

Notes

B Bankers and investors had overlooked the fact that the economic boom was being fuelled by highly risky speculative lending.

Notes

C At the same time as the US has suffered internal financial turmoil, the emergence of strong economies in other nations has undermined US economic primacy.

Notes

D As emergent economies continue to grow off the back of manufacturing and high-tech skills, it seems likely that they will pose an increasing threat to American economic might.

Notes

> Adverbs can be used to modify the meaning of a sentence, emphasizing a writer's opinion when describing a study or source.
>
> ***Example***
>
> *Denman's study was **particularly broad**, gathering results from a total of 9,000 workers in 200 US businesses, which demonstrated an overwhelming feeling among US office staff that email was a primary workplace stressor.*

5b Complete the table below with the adjectives in the box to form common collocations. Some adjectives can collocate with more than one adverb.

complex   critical   important   impressive   interesting   relevant   significant
sound   suspect   thorough   useful   valuable

greatly	particularly	especially	highly	extremely

Investigating

By the end of Part C you will be able to:

- identify the grammatical structure of reporting verbs
- identify reporting verb collocations.

1 Identifying the grammatical structure of reporting verbs

1a Work in pairs to discuss these questions.

1 Do you use the Internet to help you learn English? Why / why not?

2 Which websites would you recommend for learning English? Why?

1b Write down what your partner told you using *say* and *tell*.

Notes
1
2

1c Work in pairs to discuss these questions.

1 What is different about the grammatical structure of *say* and *tell*?

2 Could you use *say* and *tell* in an academic essay? Why / why not?

1d Dictionaries give some useful advice about the grammar of reporting verbs. Look at these examples. Use the dictionary entries to complete the table on p.24 on the use of these verbs. Think about:

- collocations
- use of *that*
- what structures can follow the reporting verb.

claim *verb* (SAY)

Definition

- [T] **to say that something is true or is a fact, although you cannot prove it and other people might not believe it**

[+ *(that)*] *Green (2006)* **claims (that)** *air pollution is not a major factor.*

[+ *to* + verb] *He* **claims to** *have found a close relationship between them, but the study has been criticized by a number of people.*

All parties have **claimed success** *in yesterday's elections.*

An unknown terrorist group has **claimed responsibility** *for this morning's bomb attack.*

identify *verb*

Definition

- [T] **to recognize a problem, need, fact, etc. and to show that it exists**

Trevor (2008) **identifies** *a number of training* **needs** *for new teachers.*

She was first to **identify** *the importance of chromosomes in inherited medical conditions.*

demonstrate *verb* (SHOW)

Definition

- [T] **to show; to make clear**

Bolero (2008) **clearly demonstrates** *the size of the economic problem facing the country.*

[+ that] Research by Passant (2005) has **demonstrated that** *babies can recognize their mother's voice very soon after birth.*

These problems **demonstrate** *the importance of strategic planning.*

Source: adapted from the *Cambridge Advanced Learner's Dictionary*

Reporting verb	Information
claim	
demonstrate	
identify	

1e In an academic context, reporting verbs are often used with an author's name. Complete the table on p.25 with these six sentences, which come from different essays. An example has been given to help you.

1 Jones (2007) believes that students at home should be aware of time-management strategies.

2 Harris (2001) stresses the importance of using VLEs in studying.

3 Aslanov (2009) reveals how students could save money by studying online.

4 Kramer (2002) advises students to make more use of online sources.

5 Bennett (2009) proposes using more interview-based data.

6 Snook (2007) considers computer-aided learning vital for student success.

Reporting structure	Example	Example reporting verbs
verb + noun phrase	2	stress
verb + *that* clause		
verb + *wh-* word		
verb + object + noun phrase		
verb + present participle		
verb + object + infinitive		

1f Add these reporting verbs to the correct part of the table in 1e. Use a dictionary to help you if necessary. Some words can appear in more than one category.

argue   cite   claim   demonstrate   find   investigate

note   offer   question   report   show

1g Complete these sentences using a suitable reporting verb from 1e and 1f in an appropriate tense. More than one correct answer is possible.

Example
Petit (2001, p.292) **offers** *a view of true workplace success as high achievement; in other words, achieving something beyond satisfying basic job requirements.*

1 For example, Harmon (ibid) _____ that office workers who were taught to use all of the features of common word-processing and office-management packages to their fullest were able to improve work rates by up to 25%, as well as cutting down on excess printing and overtime.

2 Bateman (2009) _____ that the quality of these free packages has now improved to the extent that they present a serious threat to commercial word-processing software businesses.

3 Wing et al. (2005) _____ that some popular units differ from accurate readings by as much as ten metres.

4 Some recent studies (e.g. Bardelli, 2007; Jones, 2008a) _____ the effectiveness of Open Source word-processing software packages.

5 The current paper _____ the strength of the existing claims and aims to demonstrate that the anomaly is not sufficiently explained by existing theories.

6 Diamond (1997) _____ that computer security depends on individual behaviour rather than technical solutions. However, we take the view that the increasing sophistication of hacker attacks makes strong technical security measures necessary.

7 Seminal studies such as Becher (1989) have clearly _____ the way different academic disciplines build, shape and express meaning.

8 Newman (2001) _____ that monographs are used more frequently (and earlier for undergraduate students) in the 'soft' disciplines.

9 Friedman (2007) _____ the example of skilled computer workers in India.

10 Cubrell (2004) argues that password security is a vital issue, though Morris and Irwin (2009) _____ it less important.

1h Read this extract from a text on internet security and identify the main idea.

> Recent studies into the risk to personal information on the Internet have **1)** _____
> that one of the most significant security threats is deliberate theft of personal information,
> caused by spyware and phishing scams (Mazzi & Tills, 2007; Prewitt, 2009; Wharton &
> Maas, 2003). A different position about internet threats can be found in Ison and Roth (2009),
> who **2)** _____ that the risk from spyware and phishing is actually exaggerated.
> Many home internet surfers feel that they are insufficiently knowledgeable to protect
> themselves against increasingly sophisticated attacks by online criminals. Poor awareness of
> how spyware operates has often been **3)** _____ as a reason why people magnify its
> importance as a threat. In one study of 2000 home internet users in the US (Pask, 2008, p.272),
> 87% of respondents had only the most general idea of how spyware actually worked, but 92%
> **4)** _____ it 'a very serious threat'. Sensational media stories have likewise been
> **5)** _____ as the source of this fear (Croft, 2008; Roth, 2007).
>
> Contrary to the position of Mazzi and Tills (ibid) and others, our paper **6)** _____
> that the perception of risk from spyware is indeed exaggerated by comparison both with the
> number and the severity of attacks. We **7)** _____ that a considerably more serious
> risk is posed by misuse of personal information by companies or organizations that are actually
> in legal possession of one's information for business purposes.

1i Work in pairs. Each gap in the text (1–7) can be completed with a reporting verb. First, find the subject of each verb and underline it. Then, discuss which reporting verb would be best for each gap.

1j Work with another pair and complete the text with the reporting verb you all agree is most suitable (more than one verb may be correct).

2 Identifying reporting verb collocations

> When learning a word, it is important to pay attention to the words and phrases it collocates with – that is, the words or phrases which commonly precede or follow a word in context.
>
> **Example**
>
> *It is also <u>important</u> to **cite** the extensive <u>literature</u> which describes the impact of internet availability on educational achievement.*
>
> In this example, *cite* commonly collocates with *important* and *literature*.

2a Complete this table with other collocates of the verb *cite* in the extracts on p.27 (1–5). An example has been given to help you.

	Preceding word or phrase	Tense of keyword	Following word or phrase
1	often	present perfect (passive)	as a reason why
2			
3			
4			
5			

1 Poor awareness of how spyware operates has often been cited as a reason why people magnify its importance as a threat.

2 Finally, to cite stress as a reason for choosing not to adopt email seems unrealistic.

3 For arguments in favour of teaching children to use the Internet in primary school, one could cite as an example the wider general knowledge, and broader interests, that children will acquire and develop with access to online information.

4 Dymova defended the argument by citing Ellis's early work carried out in the 1970s.

5 To support this view, we cite Palmer's claim that greater access to the Internet is beneficial.

2b Work in pairs. Look at the table you completed in 2a and discuss these questions.

1 Which kinds of word follow *cite*?

2 Which words precede *cite*?

3 Can you identify any recurring grammatical structures with *cite*?

4 Do you find this useful? Why / why not?

2c Work in groups. Each of you should choose a different reporting verb. Find five examples of each reporting verb used in context to complete this table. Use electronic texts and the search function on your computer to help you. Then report back your findings to the group.

	Preceding word or phrase	Tense of keyword	Following word or phrase
1			
2			
3			
4			
5			

> **LESSON TASK**   **3 Reporting other people's ideas**

3a You have been asked to write an academic essay with this title:

The increasing use of the Internet in developed countries has had a devastating impact on more traditional forms of communication and mass media. Identify the main areas of impact and discuss any problems that have resulted from this.

Work in small groups. Brainstorm a list of traditional forms of communication and mass media which may have been affected by increased internet use and make a list of possible problems that may have been caused by this in the table on p.28.

Main areas of impact	Resulting problems

3b Compare your ideas with another group.

3c Work in pairs. Read the extracts below from essays by students writing on the topic in 3a. Each extract is a paraphrase of a relevant source. For each one, discuss:

- which reporting verb(s) from this box would be possible in each gap
- whether the reporting verb(s) must be followed by *that*
- whether the reporting verb(s) should be singular or plural
- what tense the reporting verb(s) could be in.

> argue believe claim confirm consider establish examine hold
> investigate note observe point out reveal state suggest

1 Bryant (2005) _____ , in the G8 countries in general, the volume of post delivered has fallen annually by 5% since the late 1990s.

2 Cranston and Farago (2004) _____ the reason for the decline in television viewing in teenagers is not related to internet usage but to the rise in popularity of video gaming.

3 Munford (2009) _____ sales of DVDs reached their peak in the year 2007 and that since then they have fallen consistently across the world, with a particular slump in late 2008 and 2009.

4 In their research looking at internet user habits of over 2,000 US teenagers, Graham et al. (2008) _____ the link between time online and social communication.

5 Harbin (2006) _____ email has not only replaced the postal letter as a major form of written communication, but that it has also transformed the language people use to communicate with each other.

3d Listen to a seminar discussion on the following topic. As you listen, write notes on the opinions and positions of three of the students.

1.9

How has the spread of communications technology affected cultures around the world? Assess the extent to which the Internet is a medium for Western culture alone.

Lucy	
Simon	
Sergei	

3e Compare your notes from 3d with a partner. Then write one sentence for each of the three students in this table summarizing their position. Use an appropriate reporting verb and a different grammar structure for each person.

Type of reporting verb	Summary of speaker's position
Verb + noun phrase	
Verb + *that* clause	
Verb + *wh-* word	
Verb + present participle	
Verb + object + infinitive	

4 Review and extension

4a This table contains useful vocabulary for expressing claims and arguments. Complete it by writing the correct form(s) of the words. Leave a blank if there is no appropriate word for a particular space.

Noun	Verb	Adjective
	assume	
	cite	
	contend	
declaration		
description		
	discuss	
	emphasize	
examination		
	identify	
implication		
	infer	

		investigative
	maintain	
proposal		
	recommend	
reference		
	refine	
		revealing
	state	
summary		

4b Find and underline the reporting verb structures in these sentences. Then list three other reporting verbs that would also be suitable to report the same information.

Sentences	Reporting verb function
1 As part of his research into teenage delinquency, Mansell (2003) discovered that there was little correlation between time spent playing video games and poor behaviour.	
2 Although the data has yet to be confirmed by independent tests, Randall (2005) suggests that violent behaviour in video games does not permanently harm younger players.	
3 French (2006) argues strongly that 'online colonialism' is having a devastating effect on local culture, especially in poorer parts of the world.	
4 Although Newsome and Stonehouse (2009) maintain that the Internet encourages political activity at a local level, there is little evidence for this.	
5 Contrary to the position of Mazzi and Tills (2007) and others, our paper finds that the perception of risk from spyware is indeed exaggerated by comparison both with the number and the severity of attacks.	

Reporting in speech

By the end of Part D you will be able to:
- identify rise and fall tones for checking and adding new information
- identify and use tones for authority and finishing a topic.

1 Identifying rise and fall tones for checking and adding new information

1a Work in pairs. Read this unpunctuated sentence, which is a request from a student. Which words would you expect to receive the most prominent stress?

> excuse me could you help me

1b Read the written representation below of the same request and answer these questions.

1 Why do you think some parts of words are written in CAPITAL letters?

2 What do you think // represents?

> // exCUSE me // could you HELP me //

English, like some other languages, is spoken with intonation and stress in such a way that it can be heard as a series of 'units' or 'chunks'. These are sometimes called *tone units*. Each of the tone units in the question above is marked //. This // usually marks a small pause or a change in tone. These changes can be very small but listening out for them can help you to improve your own speaking.

1c How could you divide this request into tone units?

> could you give me some advice on what I need to do for my presentation

1d Listen to the sentence in 1c and identify:
- the syllables with the most prominent stress
- where the tone units are
- whether the tone in each unit rises or falls.

1e Listen to a dialogue between a student and his tutor and answer these questions.

1 What does the student want to know?

2 What advice does the tutor give the student?

1f Listen again and answer these questions. Does the intonation rise or fall when the:

1 tutor gives the student advice?

2 student checks that he has understood the tutor's advice?

3 tutor confirms that the student has understood the advice correctly?

1g Complete this text on the use of rise and fall tones with the words in the box.

checking   fall (×2)   rise   new

The student asked for advice on giving a presentation, so the tutor gave him information about it which the student didn't know before. The tutor used a **1)** _____ tone when giving this **2)** _____ information. **3)** _____ tones were used when the student was **4)** _____ the information, and the tutor agreeing. A **5)** _____ in tone was used to indicate the final item in the checking list.

1h Work in pairs. Read this dialogue aloud with a partner. Practise getting the stress and intonation right. If you can, record the conversation and listen to yourself. Can you identify fall and rise tones?

Student: Excuse me, where's the library from here?

Passer-by: Not too far. Keep walking along this road. Take the – let me see – the second turning on the right, and the library is a large building at the far end of the street. I think it's Smith Street.

Student: So I keep walking.

Passer-by: Yes.

Student: Take the second right.

Passer-by: Yes.

Student: And it's at the end of the street.

1i Listen and compare.

1.12

2 Identifying and using tones for authority and finishing a topic

1.13

2a Listen to a tutor greeting her class at the beginning of a lesson and complete her speech with the words you hear. Use one word in each gap only.

1) _____ **2)** _____ !
Everyone OK?
Last **3)** _____ , we looked at the **4)** _____ of **5)** _____
6) _____ .
Did you remember to **7)** _____ Chapter **8)** _____ ?

2b Listen again to identify which parts of the tutor's greeting use a rise tone, and which parts use a fall tone. Then compare your answers with a partner.

1.14

2c Listen to the rest of the tutor's introduction to the lesson, and mark the fall and rise tones.

Today, we're going to discuss it, so if you didn't, you might find today's lesson rather difficult. First of all, if you go into pairs, just quickly remind each other of what Chapter 5 is about. I'll give you three minutes.

2d Work in pairs.

1 Find and highlight at least two tone units which are at the end of a topic. What do you notice?

2 Find at least two tone units where the tutor shows they are in a position of authority. What do you notice?

2e Complete the information below on the use of rise and fall tones with the words in the box.

authority   end   fall   rise

The tutor uses **1)** _____ tones for signalling the **2)** _____ of a topic. She uses **3)** _____ tones for **4)** _____ , e.g. when she wants the students to listen.

2f Work in pairs. Read this extract from the introduction to a lecture on computer ownership and the use of the Internet. Discuss where you think the speaker is likely to use fall and rise tones, and why.

> Computer ownership is on the rise, with a recent survey by the International Telecommunications Union suggesting that there is one computer for every 76 people in the UK. I suppose that none of us are surprised that there is an attendant rise in internet activity, with a 2009 study by the Office of National Statistics indicating that about 70% of all UK homes have access to the Internet.

2g Now listen to the extract and try to identify the fall and rise tones the speaker uses.

1.15

2h Work in pairs. Can you identify any examples of:
- authoritative tone in the text?
- tone which appears at the end of a topic?

> **LESSON TASK** **3 Identifying phrases used in a group presentation**

3a Work in small groups. Read the situation below and work together to discuss the question that follows on p.34.

A university has decided to modernize its campus and the education it offers. They are planning to:
- scan and digitize all existing paper books and journals in the library
- sell off or throw away all the hard copies of books and journals
- redesign the library as a 'knowledge and learning centre' that will consist of computers with access to the Internet and the university's intranet
- video all lectures and put them online
- replace visiting lecturers with video-conferencing
- deliver assignments via email and / or mobile attachments only.

What are the advantages and disadvantages of modernizing a university in this way? Think about the effects on students, academic and non-academic staff and the local community.

3b Make notes summarizing the main points you discussed with your group. Then compare your notes with another student from the same group.

Notes
Advantages
Disadvantages

3c In your groups, prepare to present your findings in a four-minute presentation. Organize your ideas and decide who is doing which part. Produce an outline of your presentation using this table.

Introduction and outline	
Advantages	
Disadvantages	
Conclusion	

3d In this table, write down example phrases you will use in your presentation. Mark the stresses, pauses and fall or rise tones, depending on whether the phrases give 'new' information, repeat / check 'old' information, give authority or end a topic.

Function of phrase	Phrases with stresses, pauses and intonation
Introduction to topic and members	
Outline and organization	
Introduction to section	
Giving information about advantages / disadvantages	
Conclusion to section	
Conclusion and summing up	

3e Listen to another group's presentation. Each of you focus on one of the speakers and make notes in these areas.

Did the speaker ...	Yes	No	Examples
use fall tones?			
use rise tones?			
use pauses?			
use appropriate stress?			
speak directly to the audience?			
link their part to the previous / next speaker?			

3f Give individual feedback, pointing out two good features and one area to work on.

4 Review and extension

4a In English, almost any word can be stressed, depending on the meaning. Read these examples aloud. How do the different stressed words change the meaning?

1 could you GIVE me // some adVICE // on what I NEED to do // for my presenTAtion //

2 could you give ME // SOME advice // on what I need to do // for MY presentation //

3 could YOU give me // some adVICE // on WHAT I need to do // for my presenTAtion //

4b Work in pairs. Write your own short dialogue (four or five short turns) on one of these topics.

- A student asking a tutor about handing in an essay and checking the information given
- A student asking another student to clarify what homework needs doing and checking the information
- A tutor asking a student what progress they have made with preparing a presentation and checking the responses
- A group presentation speaker introducing members of the presentation team to an audience that knows them well

4c Now annotate the dialogue with appropriate tone units, and fall or rise tones. Remember what you have learned about fall / rise tones for 'new' information, checking information, authority and finishing a topic.

4d Give your dialogue to a pair of students in your next lesson to practise. Are they able to deliver the dialogue in the way you imagined it?

Reporting in writing

By the end of Part E you will be able to:

- identify general–specific structure in introductions
- identify linking words used in introductions
- write and paraphrase definitions using academic nouns.

1 Identifying general–specific structure in introductions

1a Work in pairs and discuss these questions.

- On average, roughly how many times a day do you check your email?
- Do you think that email is a convenient way to communicate? Why / why not?
- Do you think that email is an effective way to communicate? Why / why not?

1b Introductions to academic essays often have six common features. Complete the descriptions below of the features using the phrases in the box.

| aims of the essay | structure of the essay | facts or ideas |
| key vocabulary or ideas | position | background information to the topic |

- Outline of the **1)** _____
- Supporting **2)** _____
- Summary of the **3)** _____
- A statement of the author's **4)** _____
- A statement of the **5)** _____
- Definition(s) of **6)** _____

1c Read this introduction to an essay on the use of email in the context of English-language education and identify examples of the six features described in 1b.

1 Introduction

Although email has been in existence since the 1970s (Naughton, 2002, p.147), it is noticeable that there appears to be very little mention of email in contemporary English language course books. Even when they are included, the example emails given – either resembling letters or short business models – often seem very different from the emails which people actually send. Furthermore, course books give very little guidance on how to write effective emails. Perhaps this lack of attention towards emails is due to the perceived difficulty in establishing any rules; email has been described as 'a strange blend of writing and talking' (Naughton, 2002, p.143). This essay is concerned with the use of language in business and academic emails. It aims to outline the characteristic features of business email as it is actually written, and identify the differences between these and typical models of emails in course books. I suggest that the language used differs considerably, and in many different ways, depending on whether the writer is writing to a co-worker or somebody holding a more senior position. The essay begins with a summary of characteristics often cited in language course books, and then compares these formal characteristics with real emails sent between staff at a language school. Finally, possible reasons for the differences are discussed.

1d Read these extracts from the introduction and complete the table. In the second column, summarize the central point of each extract using a keyword or a short phrase. Then, consider whether the information provided by the extract summarizes a general issue or provides background information. If so, write 'General' in the third column. If the extract makes a more specific or detailed point, then write 'Specific' in the third column.

Extracts	Main point	General or Specific
Although email has been in existence since the 1970s (Naughton, 2002, p.147), it is noticeable that there appears to be very little mention of email in contemporary English language course books.	Email neglected by English language course books.	General
Even when they are included, the example emails given – either resembling letters or short business models – often seem very different from the emails which people actually send. Furthermore, course books give very little guidance on how to write effective emails. Perhaps this lack of attention towards emails is due to the perceived difficulty in establishing any rules; email has been described as 'a strange blend of writing and talking' (Naughton, 2002, p.143).		
This essay is concerned with the use of language in business and academic emails. It aims to outline the characteristic features of business email as it is actually written, and identify the differences between these and typical models of emails in course books. I suggest that the language used differs considerably, and in many different ways, depending on whether the writer is writing to a co-worker or somebody holding a more senior position.		
The essay begins with a summary of characteristics often cited in language course books, and then compares these formal characteristics with real emails sent between staff at a language school. Finally, possible reasons for the differences are discussed.		

> Sentences in introductions are often organized so that they become steadily more specific. In longer introductions, paragraphs also become more specific.

1e Read the introduction to another essay about email on p.40. In the second column, summarize the main point of each paragraph using a keyword or short phrase. In the third column, decide whether the information is general or specific.

Paragraphs	Main information given	General
Since its introduction in the late 1970s, email has been so widely adopted as a medium for communication that it now plays an essential role in business and academia. It has been claimed that it would be impossible for most modern businesses to operate without it (Waldvogel, 2007). Electronic mail offers many advantages over other modes of communication, including speed, easy recovery of communication records, and task management.		
Email plays an important role in smooth interaction in the workplace, in customer relations and in academia. However, the position of email as a mode of communication is uncertain; email operates somewhere between written and spoken types of language and both can appear depending on the context in which it is used. In casual communication between friends, it is common for email to exhibit language features which are more characteristic of casual spoken communication, while in business or academic contexts there is an expectation that the mode of communication should be more formal. Interestingly, this can present problems when a casual modality is used inappropriately in a formal context. A study of reader reactions to apparently inappropriate emails can provide important insights into the formality levels that academic staff expect students to use in communication, and therefore help to reduce misunderstandings caused by language use. Stephens et al. (2009) have pointed out that academic staff may see casual language in out-of-class communication (OCC) as being problematic. Work by Badger et al. (2010) is typical of attempts by academic staff to train students in suitable politeness levels for email-mediated OCC. This expectation of formal language use from tutors, if not recognized by students, could damage student–tutor relations and reduce the students' chance of academic success.		
OCC has been defined by Martin and Myers (2006) as any course-related communication between students and tutors, both face-to-face (e.g. 'office hours', pre- and post- class discussions, and informal meetings on campus) and remote contact, for example by telephone. However, others, including Hassini (2006) and Stephens et al. (2007), have broadened this definition to include electronically-mediated communication such as email. In this essay, OCC will be used specifically to mean student–tutor interaction by email.		

This essay investigates whether style and formality of language used in student emails to their tutors can have an effect on the tutors' willingness to help with requests via email, and investigates claims by Stephens et al. (2009) that overly casual email communication can have a negative impact on student–tutor relations and even on educational outcomes for the student.

This essay will first outline the different aspects of politeness and formality in email, then attempt to predict the effects of perceived impoliteness on the willingness of tutors to respond to requests for help from their students. The final section will discuss briefly the implications of overly casual email communication for student–tutor relations.

2 Identifying linking words used in introductions

2a Work in pairs. Read these two sentences. Find at least three ways in which the writer links the sentences to make a coherent and fluent text.

1 Although email has been in existence since the 1970s (Naughton, 2002, p.147), as a tutor, I have often wondered why there appears to be very little mention of email in contemporary English language course books.

2 Even when they are included, the example emails given – either resembling letters or short business models – often seem very different from the emails which people actually send.

2b Work in small groups. Each of you should choose a different paragraph from the text in 1e. Identify as many different ways in which the writer links sentences in your paragraph. Then compare your ideas with other students in your group.

2c Use the examples you collected to complete the second column of this table. Some rows have been left blank on the next page for you to add other categories if you wish.

Type of linking word / phrase	Example	Notes
determiner	Para. 2: both written and spoken	'both' refers back to types of language
repetition		
synonyms		
contrast		
reference		

3 Writing and paraphrasing definitions using academic nouns

> In introductions, you often need to define key terms, which may be very specialized. This means your definition needs to be clear enough for a non-specialist to understand.

3a Write a definition of *computer literacy*.

Computer literacy ...

3b Work in pairs. Compare the grammatical structure of your definitions. Does your or your partner's definition include:

- a relative clause?
- a participle clause?
- a verb in the passive voice?

3c Read these extracts from two different student essays (A and B), which provide a definition of computer literacy using the same source. Then identify the differences between A and B by completing the table below.

A Computer literacy is commonly defined as 'the ability to understand how computers work and use specific software to perform tasks' (Harmon, 1998, p.116).

B Harmon (1998) suggests that a common definition of computer literacy is the understanding of computer operation, together with the skills associated with using software.

A	B	Grammatical difference
commonly	common	adverb → adjective
defined		
to understand		
how computers work		
use ... software		

3d Rewrite these extracts in your own words.

1 *Open source* is defined as any software for which the source code is made freely available online, thus making payment to a copyright-holding company unnecessary (Braine, 1996).

Notes

2 However, if we take 'success' to mean more than simply performing one's basic job requirements, computer literacy can be seen to be a powerful booster of work efficiency (Petit, 2001).

Notes

3 Virtual conferences are a powerful tool for business professionals and involve using information technology to overcome problems created by distance, by allowing participants from all over the world to communicate with each other in real time (Nagae, 2003).

Notes

3e Work in pairs and compare your answers.

> **LESSON TASK** **4 Organizing introductions**

4a Work in pairs. How would you define *westernization*?

4b A student is preparing an essay on the following title (from Unit 1 of *Skills for Study Level 3*) and, during her research, has found the source on p.44. Read the essay title, then decide whether you think the source would be relevant or not.

How has the spread of communications technology affected cultures around the world? Assess the extent to which the Internet is a medium for Western culture alone.

Westernization is the process under which societies come under the influence of or adopt Western culture in such matters as industry, technology, law, politics, economics, lifestyle, diet, language, alphabet, religion, philosophy and / or cultural values. Westernization has been a pervasive and accelerating influence across the world in the last few centuries. Although westernization may be forced or voluntary depending on the situation of the contact, it is usually a two-sided process, in which Western influences and interests are encouraged by parts of the affected society to change towards a more westernized way of life, with the expectation of attaining some aspects and benefits of it.

Source: Russell, T. (2005). When cultures clash: the whirlpool effect. *Journal of Cultural Studies*, *32* (3), pp.23–35

4c Write a definition of *westernization*, paraphrasing key information from Russell (2005).

Notes

4d Compare your paraphrased definition with a partner. What information did you include in your definitions? What did you omit? Give reasons.

4e Ignoring the gaps for now, read this introduction to an academic essay on the spread of westernization and identify the main parts of the introduction from 1b. Which parts are missing?

The rapid spread of the Internet in the last years of the 20th century saw a renewal of the fear, in some quarters, that it would mean a creeping spread of westernization and the further erosion of local cultures around the world. **1)**_____, Western is taken to mean, essentially, that culture originating in northern Europe, **2)**_____ therefore the US and Australia–New Zealand. **3)**_____ two of **4)**_____ are geographically not western, few would dispute their rightful place in the 'Western' club. **5)**_____ to be sympathetic to the claim of a one-way flow of Western culture through the medium of the Internet when one considers the apparent evidence of this westernization: teenagers the world over drinking Coca-Cola, listening to global brand name bands from the US, Australia and Europe, **6)**_____ mimicking dress styles and behaviours that are fundamentally alien in their own cultures; politicians and business leaders from all nations using common, often US-led, models of 'best practice'. **7)**_____, it is important not to confuse globalization – which is undoubtedly being assisted in its development by the Internet and other advanced communications technology – with westernization. **8)**_____ I will attempt to show that the spread of globalization through the Internet is having a paradoxical effect: **9)**_____ a vehicle for Western values which is overwhelming non-Western cultures, the Internet is **10)**_____ helping to strengthen **11)**_____ local cultures and **12)**_____ prevent globalization from being merely a 'westernizing' phenomenon.

4f Complete the introduction in 4e with the words and phrases in the box.

> actually   although   as well as   far from being   however
>
> in this essay   in this essay   including   indeed   it seems easy
>
> these   those

4g The words and phrases in 4f are all examples of linkers. Underline other ways the writer has used to create a fluent and coherent text.

4h Compare your answers with a partner.

5 Review and extension

5a Underline the correct linking words in each of these essay extracts. In some cases, both may be possible.

1 *Although / Despite* a wide number of GPS devices are available on the market, their accuracy and reliability can vary widely.

2 There are three reasons why computer literacy should be taught in school. *At first / Firstly*, students must be able to compete with their peers in other countries …

3 Computerization of the workplace is now widespread, and, *as a consequence / as a rule*, career success depends to an extent on computer literacy.

4 The threat from viruses and spyware is often exaggerated. *Indeed / Thus* identity theft using spyware is relatively rare.

5 Modern business success owes a great deal to the spread of modern communications systems, *in detail / in particular* the development of the Internet.

6 Ownership of mobile phones among the young is growing rapidly. *As a matter of fact / Apart from this*, it is now common to see primary school children with their own mobile phones.

7 Email, despite being identified as a cause of stress, is unlikely to disappear from the modern workplace. *After all / Besides*, it is a powerful tool for instant communication.

5b These sentences (a–i) are taken from the introductions to two different essays. First, identify the sentences which belong to each introduction. Then reconstruct each introduction on the following page by putting the numbers in the correct order.

a Internet-based virtual e-health communities, which some estimates put as high as 30,000 in the UK (ibid), can now be seen as a kind of mental-health support tool.

b Online peer-to-peer communities allow people with shared interests to gather virtually.

c Possible explanations include gas leaks on board the spacecraft, as well as the distorting effects of heat radiation from several separate components within the craft.

d The current paper investigates the strength of the existing claims and aims to demonstrate that the anomaly is not sufficiently explained by existing theories.

e The Pioneer 10 and 11 space probes have long been known to report anomalous data (commonly known as the Pioneer Anomaly).

f This anomalous signal from the spacecraft is widely accepted (Low, 2006), but there is considerable disagreement about its cause.

g This offers benefits for healthcare workers, who can use peer-to-peer technology to help patients with similar needs share their experiences, give advice, get answers to questions and offer practical and emotional support (Waller, 2004).

h This paper will consider how effective these virtual communities are in supporting patients and their ultimate impact on health outcomes.

i The paper concludes by presenting some brief ideas about areas for further investigation of the phenomenon.

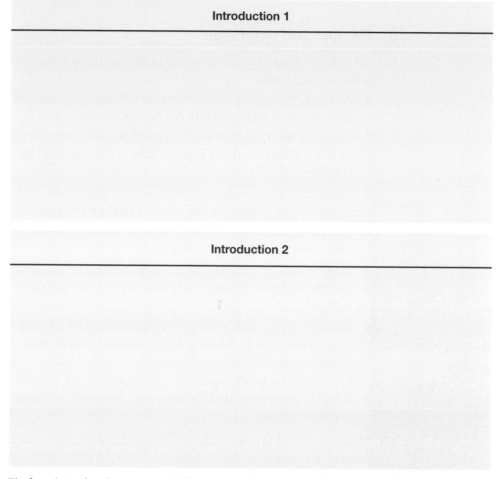

Introduction 1

Introduction 2

5c Find an introduction to an article or essay from your subject. Identify the main parts. What similarities / differences does it have in structure compared to the ones you have looked at in this section? Highlight some of the linking devices the writer(s) used.

5d Bring the introduction and your analysis of it to your next class. Be prepared to share your ideas with other students.

Unit 2 New frontiers

Unit overview

Part	This part will help you to ...	By improving your ability to ...
A	**Follow lectures in English**	• recognize and use stressed and unstressed syllables in tone units • identify lead-in and question structures.
B	**Understand written arguments**	• identify signposting for written arguments and counter-arguments • identify assumptions • identify and use word-order inversion.
C	**Clearly express and support your own stance on a topic**	• identify and use hedging devices • identify vocabulary and grammar used in stating premises.
D	**Participate in academic presentations / discussions**	• refer to graphics and visual data • refer to other sources in a presentation.
E	**Write an academic essay**	• use *it* and *this* to link between sentences • use *it* phrases to convey opinion.

Understanding spoken information

By the end of Part A you will be able to:
- recognize and use stressed and unstressed syllables in tone units
- identify lead-in and question structures.

1 Recognizing and using stressed and unstressed syllables in tone units

1a Match the names of the planets with their stress patterns in the table below.

Mercury ~~Venus~~ Earth Mars Jupiter Saturn Uranus Neptune

Stress pattern	Planets
O	
Oo	VEnus
Ooo	

1b You are going to hear part of a lecture on space and private enterprise. Before you listen, work in pairs to discuss these topics. What do you think the speaker will say about them?
- The costs / risks of space exploration
- The history of space exploration
- The control of space exploration
- Recent changes in space exploration

2.1

1c Listen to the lecture. Did you and your partner raise similar points to the speaker?

1d Here is an extract from the lecture. Where do you think the stressed syllables are?

Space has often been called a new frontier for humankind. It is a region of great risk, and both human and financial cost, but it is also a region of great opportunity. The history of human space exploration began very recently, in space terms anyway, with Yuri Gagarin's orbit of the Earth in 1961. Since then, it's largely been the sole preserve of various national government agencies, often involving the military.

The most common unstressed sound in English is schwa /ə/, often described as 'lax', meaning that it does not take much effort to articulate. To find out if a weak syllable contains /ə/, you will need to look at spelling, as /ə/ is linked to certain vowels and vowel combinations.

2.2

1e Listen to these two sentences, paying particular attention to the /ə/ sound.

      /ə/ /ə//ə/   /ə/   /ə//ə/   /ə/

  1 It is a region of great risk, and both human and financial cost.

                /ə/ /ə/ /ə//ə/   /ə/   /ə//ə/   /ə/

  2 Space is certainly a region of great risks and costs, both human and financial.

1f Work in pairs. Mark the tone units in the sentences with //.

1g Practise saying the tone units, paying attention to the schwa sounds.

2 Identifying lead-in and question structures

2a Work in pairs to discuss these questions.

  1 Why do members of the audience ask questions during or at the end of a presentation?

  2 What sorts of question are usually asked?

  3 When asking a question at the end of a presentation, what background information might the questioner need to give to the speaker?

2b These questions were all asked at the end of a presentation on the development of space. Match the three different parts of each question, A, B and C.

A	B	C
1 I wonder if	common access to space	for most people to go into space if the cost is so high?
2 How does	it will be impossible	that might be useful?
3 Don't you think	that costs of space travel	affect your claim that only trained military pilots are suitable astronauts?
4 Are you suggesting	of any further research in this area	how long periods in space would affect family life.
5 Do you know	you could comment on	will be about twenty times lower within a decade?

2.3

2c Listen to the questions and check your answers.

It can be helpful to explain the background to your question before asking it. This is known as a *lead-in* to the question.

Example

You mentioned that the costs of privately run space vehicles will be much lower than those for government spaceflight programmes. *Do you have any data or evidence to support this?*

2d Work in pairs. Discuss why it is useful to use a lead-in before asking a question.

2e You are going to examine the grammatical structures of certain lead-ins to questions that you could ask at the end of presentations or lectures. Read the questions below. Underline the lead-in, circle the referring word(s) in the question, then identify what the referring word(s) refers to.

Example

'You mentioned that private space travel is likely to develop to the point where some workers will be spending long periods in space. I wonder if you could comment on how (that) would affect family life.' = *long periods in space*

1 'The 2003 UN report on the development of space says that no military activity should be allowed there. How does this affect your claim that only trained military pilots are suitable astronauts?'

2 'You mentioned that space travel is enormously expensive, but then you said that you still think it's possible for private companies. Don't you think it will be impossible for most people if the cost is so high?'

3 'I'm sorry, I didn't understand your point about travel costs in space. Are you suggesting that they will be about twenty times lower within a decade?'

4 'I'm not sure I fully agree with your point on the negative impact of humankind in space. Do you know of any further research in this area that might be useful?'

2f This is the structure of the lead-in and question for the example in 2e. The type of question is noted in the third column.

Lead-in	Question structure	Type of question
You *mentioned that* + clause	*I wonder if* + *you could* + verb	Enquiry

Here are four more question types:

clarification	decision aid	disputation	synthesis

Complete this table with the lead-ins and questions from 2e.

	Lead-in	Question structure	Type of question
1			
2			
3			
4			

3a Work in pairs to discuss these questions.

- What's the most exotic place you've ever visited?
- Would you prefer to go on a camping trip or stay in a hotel? Why?
- Would you enjoy a trip to a remote island to see an isolated tribal community? Why / why not?

2.4

3b Listen to an extract from a lecture on ethno-tourism. Write down details about the tribal communities that the speaker mentions.

3c Share the information in your notes with a partner. Then think of questions you might like to ask the lecturer based on what you have heard. Make a note of your questions on a piece of paper.

3d Listen and complete this lead-in and question.

2.5

1) _____ _____ _____ there are tribes who have never had recorded contact with outsiders. Don't **2)** _____ _____ _____ _____ _____ _____ to have no contact with the modern world?

3e Work in pairs to discuss what kind of question it is (enquiry, disputation, etc.).

3f Listen to the lecture extract in 3b again and complete this table with two more questions about the information, one enquiry and one disputation.

Type of question	Lead-in	Question
Enquiry		
Disputation		

2.6

3g Listen to the next part of the lecture. Write notes on the benefits and problems associated with life in isolated communities.

Notes
Benefits
Problems

2.7

3h Listen and complete this question based on these benefits / problems.

A recent UN report on tribal groups says that they are vulnerable to disease. How does this _____ modernity bringing advanced medical care?

3i Work in pairs to discuss what kind of question it is (enquiry, disputation, etc.).

3j Use your notes from 3g to write two more questions about the benefits and problems associated with life in isolated communities, one asking for more information, one asking for clarification.

Type of question	Lead-in	Question
Synthesis		
Clarification		

3k Work in groups. Make a list of:

- specific ways that tribal groups can benefit from the profits of ethno-tourism
- specific ways that tourists can benefit from contact with local tribes
- how ethno-tourism companies should behave towards tribal groups.

2.8

3l Now listen to a longer extract and write notes on the information given on the topics you discussed in 3k.

3m Work in pairs. Use your notes from this section to write four questions you could ask the lecturer about ethno-tourism.

Type of question	Lead-in	Question structure

3n Work in pairs.

Student A: You are a student, asking one of the questions you listed in 3j and 3m.

Student B: You are the lecturer. Try to answer Student A's question, using the notes you've made in this section.

Then change roles and select a different question.

4 Review and extension

4a A wealthy business-person has just returned from a two-week tourist trip to the International Space Station. Read some of the comments that the space tourist made about their trip. Then think of some questions that you could ask them about their mission, using the indirect lead-ins you studied in Sections 2 and 3.

1 'It takes a while for your body to adjust. I spent about three days being sick at first. Some people feel OK very quickly, but others can be sick for up to a week.'

2 'Sleeping is the hardest part. It's actually very comfortable, but really, really noisy, because of fans and other equipment running all the time. And of course you're excited, so you feel pretty sleep-deprived after a while.'

3 'From space, looking down on the Earth, you realize just how thin the atmosphere is. There's this huge planet and just this tiny, thin atmosphere.'

4 'I think there's great opportunity for private enterprise in space, whether it's for tourism or commercial industry, or even exploration. I think private companies, over the next few decades, are going to achieve amazing things in space.'

5 'There's a great sense of community among the crew, even though we're all from different countries. Most people either speak Russian or English, because we all have language courses during our training, and we communicate just fine.'

4b A professional astronaut has just given a lecture; at the end, they are asked some questions. Complete the lead-ins and questions below with the phrases in the box.

a Don't you think they would

b mentioned before that you would never

c haven't there

d there anything you would like to be

e mentioned earlier how Earth

f there anything

g Will that be

h you think its appearance has

i Don't you think that would be too

1 You _____ go back into space. Why is that?

2 You _____ looked from space. Do _____ changed since global warming started?

3 You mentioned plans by NASA to return to the Moon. _____ expensive in this time of economic crisis?

4 You suggested humans would live on Mars one day. _____ within our lifetime?

5 There have been many discoveries in space, _____ ? Which do you think has been the most important?

6 Many people in this hall believe in UFOs and extraterrestrials. _____ already be here if there were any?

7 You mentioned not being afraid of going into space. Was _____ you were worried about?

8 You touched upon retirement. Is _____ remembered for?

4c Now check your answers by listening to the lead-ins and questions from the audience.

2.9

Understanding written information

By the end of Part B you will be able to:
- identify signposting for written arguments and counter-arguments
- identify assumptions
- identify and use word-order inversion.

1 Identifying signposting for written arguments and counter-arguments

1a Read the extract below from an introduction to an academic text about ethno-tourism. Identify which sentences state:

1 the writer's argument / position

2 possible counter-arguments to their argument / position.

> Ethno-tourism should benefit both the visitors and the contacted tribal communities. However, many recent studies strongly assert the negative impact of ethno-tourism on the subject communities. In this paper, I examine how these claims actually exaggerate the negative consequences of contact with tourists and the tourism industry, without fully considering the positive impact of these ventures.

1b Complete this table with the signposting that helped you decide.

Common signposting for introducing arguments and counter-arguments

1c Here are seven other statements that either present the argument that ethno-tourism is beneficial, or the counter-argument that it is mainly negative. Work in pairs to decide whether the writer is stating an argument / position (AP) or counter-argument (CA). Then add any signposting that helped you decide to the table above.

1 Critics of ethno-tourism oppose the use of recently contacted (or 'uncontacted') tribal communities for commercial purposes.

2 A further complaint aimed at ethno-tourism is its effect on the cohesion of the contacted communities.

3 Pedersen (2009) has argued that the risk of death from disease is such that we have a moral responsibility to leave these people in peace.

4 Some supporters of responsible tourism argue that well-managed tourism programmes can avoid the effects of social breakdown.

5 This paper seeks to address the question of how well ethno-tourism can benefit local communities and suggests that this can only be done effectively if the local communities themselves are involved in the decision-making process.

6 The negative impacts of ethno-tourism can be great, and while it is certainly undeniable that these can, and have, destroyed whole cultures, nevertheless I will argue that ethno-tourism is still of great benefit.

7 The negative view of ethno-tourism has been strongly challenged in recent years by a number of writers who suggest that socio-cultural benefits should also be considered.

Signposting helps make the reader aware of exactly what is being argued in an academic text. Another area where signposting is usually needed is when the writer is attempting to rebut counter-arguments.

1d These three extracts are from different academic texts where the writer is rebutting a counter-argument. Work in pairs to establish and briefly note what the counter-argument is, and how the writer has rebutted it in each case. Underline the key signposting each writer uses.

While we do not dispute claims that some instances exist where tribal groups have lost land rights, the extent to which this has occurred remains relatively insignificant.

Notes

Argument: Ethno-tourism benefits local communities

Counter-argument:

Rebuttal:

None of this is to deny that there are many examples of the negative consequences resulting from contact between developed world tourists and isolated tribal communities. Nevertheless, the examples presented in this paper suggest that the experience is overwhelmingly positive for both parties in the majority of instances.

Notes

Argument: There are many advantages to ethno-tourism

Counter-argument:

Rebuttal:

However, far from the popular perception that this money is well spent on exciting and innovative space research, this investment provides little return in benefits and would almost certainly be put to better use dealing with more important issues on Earth.

Notes

Argument: Space exploration is too expensive

Counter-argument:

Rebuttal:

1e Identify information in this piece of academic writing regarding the writer's argument, counter-arguments and rebuttal of the counter-arguments.

NASA has established a constant presence in space, with the permanently manned International Space Station, space-based satellites and probes, human spaceflight in near-Earth orbit and even ambitious plans to return astronauts to the Moon in the near future and then on to a pioneering mission to Mars by the middle of this century. NASA's total annual budget is approximately 13 billion dollars (Haskins, 2008). This is a huge amount, and the extent to which this money has been spent wisely needs to be questioned. **1)** _____ that despite 50 years of spaceflight, the vast amount spent has given little return in benefits, and could almost certainly be put to better use dealing with more important issues on Earth. **2)** _____ that this is money well spent on exciting and innovative space research. **3)** _____ , while this is undoubtedly true, this only makes the problem worse because even more money will then be spent on projects that do not directly benefit the growing population on this planet.

1f Use the information you identified in 1e to complete the text.

2 Identifying assumptions

2a Read this dictionary definition of *assumption*. Work in pairs to discuss why people may make assumptions about someone depending on their age.

> **assumption** *noun* /əˈsʌmpʃn/
>
> *Definition*
>
> • [C] **something that you accept as true without question or proof**
>
> *People tend to **make** assumptions **about** you depending on your age.*
>
> *These calculations are **based on** the assumption that prices will continue to rise.*

Source: the *Cambridge Advanced Learner's Dictionary*

2b Read these statements from student essays. What has the writer accepted as true in each statement? Find at least two assumptions in each one.

1 The ice cover over the Arctic will have totally disappeared in 20 years' time.

2 Young people are growing up with poor eyesight because of the availability of TV and video games in the home.

3 Space exploration is too expensive. Each rocket costs a huge amount of money.

4 The Internet is probably the easiest way of obtaining information.

2c Read these statements about video gaming. Work in pairs to discuss which statements you agree or disagree with, explaining your reasons.

• Video gaming is mainly for teenagers.

• Video gaming is largely a male pastime.

• People who play video games tend to have fewer social skills than other people.

• Video gaming is largely a waste of time.

• Video gaming is addictive.

• Video games can make young people more violent.

• Video gaming can lead to health problems.

2d You are going to read an article about video gaming. First look at the title and work in pairs to discuss if you agree with it and the assumption underlying it.

Video game advances threaten society

The video games industry is worth approximately US$48 billion (£30 billion) a year, similar to the revenue earned by Hollywood. This is remarkable when you consider that games industry revenues have increased 50% in the last three years and look set to continue rising. What's driving this boom in gaming? Three things, says Games Designers Conference organizer Ron Kricek: improvements in the quality and speed of games platforms, the spread of high-tech mobile technology, and a widening section of the population who are trying games for the first time.

2e Now read the whole paragraph and discuss what assumptions the writer makes.

2f Read a further extract from the article on video gaming. Underline any phrases which contain assumptions. An example has been given to help you.

Top-of-the-line games platforms already boast processing speeds in the range of 3 to 4 gigahertz, as well as powerful software which can render lifelike graphics and a certain level of artificial intelligence in the characters that one meets in a game. <u>Experts predict an explosion in processing power in the next decade</u>, anything between 10 and 100 gig systems, with software to match. But that's not the end of the story: at the most recent Games Designers Conference, delighted fans and developers were able to get a taste of the future of gaming – headsets which can 'read' the brainwaves of players and translate them into actions on the screen; cameras which can be mounted on top of screens and perfectly capture your movements as you play – no need for a Wii remote when the games console can simply capture your movements; even goggles which give the player complete – or near enough – immersion in a hyper-realistic game environment which only they can see.

All of this is great news for the army of gaming fans around the world – an army which is growing rapidly. Gone are the days when video games were the sole preserve of teenage boys – the popularity of the Wii, and its relatively simple games, demonstrated that just about everyone likes to play games of some sort, if given the chance. A large part of the growing games market is women, young children and the elderly, and the industry is responding by creating more games tailored to their interests. When you couple this with the revolution in mobile technology, it's possible to glimpse the future – and it's not a nice one.

When reading academic texts, assumptions can sometimes be recognized through these language features:

- absolutes (e.g. *all, always*, etc.)
- lack of caution, or lack of hedging expressions (e.g. the use of *is / are* rather than *may be*)
- the use of adverbs to (over)emphasize verbs (e.g. **completely** *disappeared* instead of *disappeared*).

2g Identify any examples of these categories you can find in the phrases you underlined in 2f.

2h Read a final extract from the article. Underline any assumptions. An example has been given to help you.

Imagine the scene on your morning commute to work – a carriage full of passengers, wearing goggles that wrap them in their own game fantasies, each absorbed in a virtual world while ignoring the world around them. <u>As games platforms improve, people will be exposed to a more realistic, and more satisfying, gaming experience</u>, and will inevitably want to spend more time in the fantasy worlds that the games offer. The result can only be the weakening of our societies, as real-world social bonds are ignored in favour of the imaginary pleasures of the game. In a world in which everyone is wrapped up in their own reality, real criminals will find it easier to prey on distracted people. When the temptation to play games is so strong that we all – kids, parents, the elderly – want to spend our time in them, what happens to family life? What happens to exercise? We risk sacrificing a better future for humanity by allowing ourselves to be hypnotized by a make-believe world.

2i Work in pairs. Compare what you have both underlined. Discuss your decisions and what language features are used, referring to the features listed above.

3   Identifying and using word-order inversion

3a   This sentence is from the article on video games. Is there anything grammatically unusual (e.g. relating to word order) about the sentence?

> Gone are the days when video games were the sole preserve of teenage boys.

3b   Rewrite the sentence in 3a using a different word order.

3c   In pairs or small groups, discuss why the writer has decided to use the inverted form.

> Word-order inversion allows some sentences to be restructured in order to provide a different emphasis. Usually this involves switching the order of the subject and the verb in a sentence.
>
> ***Examples:***
> *The dog hasn't barked once.*
> *Not once has the dog barked.*
>
> Certain phrases are often used to introduce such sentences. Some of the most common are:
>
> *Not once …   No longer …   No sooner …   At no point …*
> *Under no circumstances …*

3d   Find and underline an example of inversion in this extract from an academic essay.

> A large number of international students were interviewed as part of the research. However, under no circumstances were these interviewees asked for their name. This was so that strict anonymity could be preserved throughout.

3e   How could you rewrite the inversion you identified?

3f   Complete the sentences below, which all contain inversion, with the words in the box.

did   had   were   were

1   At no time _____ the mice under stress.
2   Not until much later _____ the results appear to confirm this.
3   No sooner _____ the results arrived than it was discovered there was a flaw.
4   Not only _____ the results what we predicted, but they correlated with other studies.

3g   Work in pairs. Rewrite the sentences in 3f without inversion.

4 Evaluating the basis of an argument

4a Work in small groups. Discuss your experiences of learning English.

- Tell each other when and why you first started learning English.
- Have your reasons changed? How? Why?
- What do you find difficult about English?
- What things do you find relatively easy?

4b Read this excerpt from a student essay about the English language. Work in pairs to discuss which aspects you agree with, and which aspects you disagree with.

English has become a global language for many reasons. Firstly, English was the language of the British Empire, which helped to establish English as a language around the world, including in Australia, India, Canada and some African states. Secondly, and maybe most importantly, America has been the dominant global power in the world over the past few decades. America also produces most of the scientific and technological advances too, which are published in English.

Universities in the UK, Australia, Canada and America are regarded as among the best in the world, and, as a result, many students travel to these countries to study, needing to learn English in order to do so.

Another reason is that more and more people can afford to travel and go on holiday. Since it is more convenient to learn one language, and with English being so widely used, many tourists find it useful to learn English.

4c Read these predictions about the future of English based on the text in 4b. Work in pairs to discuss whether you agree with them. What other predictions could be made?

1 English will be the world language in 2020.

2 English will change as different groups of people start to use it.

4d Read these paragraphs, each of which presents a premise for the argument in the text in 4b. In small groups, discuss whether you agree with the opinions in them or not. If you do agree, what evidence is there for this?

Experts predict that China will be the biggest economy in the world in ten years' time. Gone are the days of American domination. As China gets more powerful, people will have to learn Chinese. There are more Chinese speakers than English speakers, and the time will come when Chinese will become more important than English outside China.

Many English people already complain that the world is full of people who can't use English well, and this is very clear from the signs that we see. Recently I saw a sign in Norway which said 'Ladies are requested not to have children in the bar'! Different kinds of English are appearing, because one group of people, or nationality, learn English in the same way in their country and develop the same characteristics. We can expect this to happen more and more, with the result that everyone will learn a slightly different English. English will end up like Latin, splitting up into lots of different languages.

However, China is not the only powerful state that is getting richer. Various countries and regions are increasing their wealth, such as Russia, the Arab states, India and Brazil. It's clear that these countries will dominate their regions, and people living near them will have to learn that language for commercial and cultural reasons.

Because of the Internet, everyone needs to understand each other. Therefore the different 'Englishes' that some people claim are developing will become more similar, not more different. However, this 'similar' English is likely to be a business English rather than a literary English, and this will be simpler and less beautiful.

There is no reason to think the present situation will change in the near future. It's quite clear that in 20 or 30 years' time, English will be even more commonly spoken, which will lead to people not learning their own languages.

4e Work in small groups. Try to think of counter-arguments for the opinions expressed in 4d.

4f Work in new groups. Discuss your opinions. Try to provide evidence or supporting arguments for your claims.

5 Review and extension

5a Read these three claims, then rewrite the information using a word-order inversion and the starting phrases below.

1
The coming years will see remarkable improvements in healthcare as a result of advances in nanotechnology – the creation of extremely small robots which can be programmed to carry out delicate tasks which humans are unable to do.

2
I can't say I agree with claims about climate change – that our society may be destroyed by environmental damage. I mean, the forecasts say that this might happen within a couple of hundred years, but by then we will have colonized space, so it's not really all that important, is it? Our society will survive.

3
One of the key advantages of ethno-tourism is that the tribes which are contacted will be able to get the benefit of modern civilization – modern hospitals, education, housing. By bringing isolated tribes into the civilized world, we give their children the opportunity to participate in the world.

1   Not until the creation of small robots …

2   Only after we have colonized space …

3   Not only …

5b Read this text. Identify the assumptions that the author makes.

Video gaming is now a multi-billion dollar-a-year industry (Abbot, 2009), yet the negative stereotype of the 'typical' video-games player – a lone (and possibly lonely) teenage boy – remains in many quarters. This prejudice is changing only slowly as gaming becomes more popular with a broader audience, and many people are still resistant to the idea of gaming as a respectable activity for all ages and levels of society. However, within a decade, and possibly even sooner (Johanssen, 2010, p.12) we will see gaming become a mainstream activity, with broad social appeal. This will be a true revolution not unlike the mobile revolution of the early 2000s, unlocking a powerful range of human potentials which well-designed games can capture and enhance. The key to this is, as Shales et al. (2004) point out, redefining our view of games. Whereas in the past we have often dismissed games as mere recreation, we will increasingly come to see gaming as a powerful learning tool and it is this that will be the secret of its appeal.

Investigating

By the end of Part C you will be able to:

- identify and use hedging devices
- identify vocabulary and grammar used in stating premises.

1 Identifying and using hedging devices

1a Complete the table below with the different types of hedging device in the box.

adverbs of frequency *it* phrases modal adjectives modal adverbs modal nouns modal verbs reporting verbs tentative verbs *there* phrases

Hedging device	Example word / phrase
	seem
	suggest
	may
	certainty
	certain
	certainly
	often
	It is likely that
	There is a possibility that

1b Read the first paragraph from an article about in-vitro meat and underline any hedging words or expressions you find.

In-vitro cultured meat could soon be an everyday reality for millions of consumers. In-vitro meat is grown in a tank by culturing muscle cells from a living animal and enhancing them with artificial proteins. This is essentially the same technique as is already used for the production of yoghurt cultures. The ability to produce artificial meat in this way offers benefits to human health, the environment, and the welfare of animals currently bred for slaughter. However, it is a technology in its infancy, and though such meat has been successfully created in a number of experiments, no in-vitro meat is currently approved for human consumption. Important questions remain to be answered before it becomes a commonly accepted human food resource. This essay will consider arguments supporting the production of in-vitro meat, as well as those that maintain that such a method of meat production should not be pursued. The essay will conclude with this author's own view on the topic.

1c Read the next paragraph. Use the table from 1a and the prompts in brackets to suggest suitable words / phrases to complete it. Compare your answers with a partner.

Experiments in the culturing of artificial meat have been continuing since the early 1990s, originally derived from NASA interest in a source of artificial protein for long-term space flights. In-vitro cultured meat offers a **1)** _____ (*modal noun*) of benefits: it is **2)** _____ (*reporting verb*) that it is healthier than animal-grown meat, as food developers **3)** _____ (*modal verb*) control the nutritional content, in particular the fat content. A recent experiment (Olson, 2010, pp.43–44) showed that tank-grown in-vitro chicken was 80% leaner than its animal equivalent. Also, in-vitro meat is **4)** _____ (*adverb*) kinder to animals. Scientists researching the possibilities of growing artificial meat find themselves in the rather odd position of being supported by vegetarian and vegan groups, as well as animal rights campaigners who **5)** _____ (*adverb*) focus on arguing against meat consumption. In a statement to the UK Food and Biotechnology Council, a leading in-vitro researcher **6)** _____ (*reporting verb*) that current methods of intensive farming of live animals for meat production **7)** _____ (*adverb*) caused pain and distress for the animals involved. It was further **8)** _____ (*reporting verb*) that the culturing of completely artificial meat **9)** _____ (*modal verb*) be an effective answer to this, as the meat is grown without a nervous system, and therefore manufacturers are not faced with the ethical problem of causing pain (Chavez, 2009, p.108).

2 Identifying vocabulary and grammar used in stating premises

2a Work in pairs to discuss these questions.

1 What do you think a nanorobot is?

2 What do you think nanorobots could be used for?

2b Work in pairs. Read the text below about nanorobots, then answer these questions.

1 Do they exist already?

2 What is one possible way in which nanorobots can be used?

Premise(s)
Nanorobots, incredibly small robots which can be programmed to perform a variety of tasks, are nearly a reality. Scientists predict that functioning, safe nanorobots will be commonplace within five years. One important potential use for these machines is in medicine, for example with nanorobots programmed to attack cancer cells being injected into a human body.

Argument
Within five to ten years, we can expect to see a remarkable decrease in cancer rates as a result of this technological advance.

2c Discuss these words and phrases from the text. Say what effect they may have on a reader's understanding and interpretation of the text.

1 **incredibly** small

2 **nearly** a reality

3 predict that … **will be** commonplace within five years

4 **potential** use

5 we **can expect** to see

6 **as a result** of

2d Read this text about oil and gas prices and write your answers to the questions below.

Premises

Scientists believe that there may be substantial reserves of gas and oil under the Arctic Ocean seabed. Some predictions put the potential oil reserve as high as 20% of the world total, which is similar to the reserve in Saudi Arabia. The ice cover over the North Pole, which has prevented exploitation of this resource, is melting rapidly and is expected to have disappeared by mid-century.

Argument

Because of this, from 2050 onwards, oil and gas prices will fall dramatically as this new supply becomes available.

1 In the first sentence, what
   a main verbs are used?
   b tense are the verbs in?
   c does the choice of verbs suggest about the certainty of the information?

2 In the second sentence, what
   a does the use of *some* in *Some predictions* suggest about the certainty of the information?
   b comparison is made? What does it suggest about the certainty of the information?

3 In the third sentence, what
   a main verbs are used?
   b tense are the verbs in?
   c does the choice of verbs suggest about the certainty of the information?

Notes
Sentence 1:
Sentence 2:
Sentence 3:

Certainty and reliability

Usually, being certain about something is considered better than being uncertain. However, most topics suitable for academic consideration are subject to a least some debate. In this context, to appear to be certain about something that hasn't yet been agreed upon by experts in the field can suggest a lack of proper understanding. In this way, certainty that is not clearly based on overwhelming evidence can actually make a piece of academic writing less reliable.

2e Work in pairs. Read this text about internet access and libraries and discuss the extent to which you accept the writer's argument.

> **Premises**
> Internet accessibility is expanding rapidly around the globe. It is now commonplace for students to have their own internet-accessible laptops, used for research as well as writing assignments. At the same time, universities and academic publishers are increasingly making digital versions of their texts available online.
>
> **Argument**
> As a result, higher education libraries, the actual buildings where hard copies of books and journals are stored, will see fewer and fewer visitors walking through their doors and will eventually become obsolete.

2f Underline any words and phrases which make the premises and argument seem unreliable.

2g Work in pairs. Discuss what alternative words and phrases you could use to make the premises and argument appear more reliable to the reader.

2h Rewrite the text in 2e in a way which would suggest the information is more reliable.

> **LESSON TASK** 3 **Hedging an argument**

3a Work in pairs. Discuss whether you think these statements about video games are true (T) or false (F).

	True (T)	False (F)
1 More people play online video games than graduate each year from universities.		
2 Educational online video games are just as popular as entertainment games.		
3 Gaming can be an effective way to educate people.		

3b Read this introduction to a text about video games as an educational tool. Identify any differences between your answers from 3a and those in this text.

> The number of students graduating each year from universities with degrees in the hard sciences and applied subjects like engineering is dwarfed by comparison with the number of enthusiastic players of modern online video games such as *Lineage* or *Civilization*. While these games have entertainment as their explicit purpose, there is evidence that games with a deliberate instructive aim are also highly popular. *Food Force*, for instance, a game produced by the UN to teach players about food aid distribution, has several million players. A growing body of scholarly work suggests that the future of education lies in gaming. Gaming offers a singularly effective way to improve the student learning experience.

3c Read the text again. Identify any hedging expressions used.

3d Which of these expressions would the writer probably agree with?

1 Educational games are definitely as popular as entertainment-only games.

2 In the future, video games may increasingly be used for education.

3 All games in the future will be educational.

3e Work in small groups to discuss these points.

- Tell each other about any positive or negative experiences you have had (or know about from friends) of online video games.
- Do you agree that 'gaming offers a singularly effective way to improve the student learning experience'? Why / why not?
- Do you think gaming will replace more traditional forms of education? Why / why not? When?
- List at least five possible consequences if gaming replaced lectures and seminars as a method of education at higher levels.

3f Now read the rest of the text. Work in pairs to complete it with the hedging expressions in the box.

a clear	almost	almost	apparent	appear	can
	depending on	not all	perhaps	possible	

Firstly, it is important to realize that gaming-as-educational-tool is not some possibility which lies only in the distant future; a number of popular educational games designed for students in the sciences and engineering already exist. Initial studies investigating the effectiveness of these games show **1)** _____ improvement in assessment marks from students who were taught using the games compared with others who received courses by attending conventional lectures. One study recorded an average increase of over 40% on test scores in the groups learning through interactive games. However, **2)** _____ results have been as positive as this, **3)** _____ how well the games are designed. A poorly designed game **4)** _____ still clearly inhibit learning in the way that a dull series of lectures can. Learning benefits **5)** _____ to have resulted from games that incorporated effective learning practices and situations.

6) _____ reasons for the **7)** _____ superiority of games when compared to learning from a series of lectures are various. Information in a lecture is delivered in an **8)** _____ entirely aural mode, while in a game, the players / students receive input through both listening to speech or sounds in the game environment, as well as visually. An increase in the modes by which information is received has long been acknowledged to have clear learning benefits. There is more input and feedback available in a game than a lecture. Something new happens **9)** _____ every time a player presses a button during a game, giving the player feedback and new information about their environment, while students in lectures have **10)** _____ only one or two opportunities to interact with the information by asking questions. Literacy professor Paul Gee, a strong proponent of learning through video gaming, also points out that the challenges or tasks in many games need players to develop skills in thinking logically – the formation of hypotheses, experimentation, and reflecting on their performance if they fail at first. Games, far from being superficial or childish entertainment, are loaded with a variety of learning experiences.

Source: Hislop, P. (2006). *Learning and Gaming.* York: Saxon Press.

3g Work in pairs. Read this summary of the text above, then amend it by using appropriate hedging.

Hislop (2006) reports that video games used with science and engineering students are 40% more effective than lectures for learning, although the design of the games is a crucial factor in determining this. He also asserts that this is because games provide many different ways for students to gain information and feedback compared to those in lectures, and that gaming provides opportunities for hypothesis forming, experimenting with ideas and thinking about how well they have done – all essential aspects of learning.

3h Read these three premises and arguments about the use of video gaming in education. Then work in small groups, underlining any assumptions or words or phrases which make the premise or argument less reliable.

Premises

There is currently an <u>enormous</u> gap in the experience and quality of so-called 'entertainment' games and deliberately 'educational' ones. Commercial entertainment-focused games boast visually stunning graphics and exciting, often violent, scenarios, alongside pulse-raising soundtracks, often created by tie-ins with the movie and record industries. It is to this that they owe their enduring popularity and market success.

Argument

Educational games will never become as popular or as exciting to use as entertainment ones.

Premises

No standard test exists which can be applied to measure the educational effectiveness of video games. Without guarantees of the quality of the games, how will educators ever be convinced to begin using them with their students?

Argument

Educational video games are highly unlikely to replace other kinds of education.

Premises

Entertainment games released for commercial profit are backed by enormous, financially powerful software development companies which are willing to invest in future games that they know will turn profits. Educational games, on the other hand, are generally produced and distributed by interested researchers relying on higher education research funding.

Argument

Educational games will never develop to their potential due to lack of funds.

3i Critically discuss whether you agree with the argument based on each set of premises. Do you think they are logical? Why / why not? Use hedging to indicate your own level of certainty.

3j Rewrite the argument(s) to reflect your own opinions.

4 Review and extension

4a You are going to read an extract from an article on video games. Read these three sentences, noting the underlined one, then rewrite the underlined sentence below using more formal language.

The video games industry is worth approximately US$48 billion (£30 billion) a year, similar to the revenue earned by Hollywood. This is remarkable when you consider that games industry revenues have increased 50% in the last three years and look set to continue rising. <u>What's driving this boom in gaming?</u>

4b Read this extract, focusing on the underlined words, then rewrite the underlined phrase below in a more formal style.

> Three things, says Game Designers Conference organizer Ron Kricek: improvements in the quality and speed of games platforms, the spread of high-tech mobile technology, and a widening section of the population who are trying games for the first time.

4c Read this extract. Which words are metaphorical?

> Experts predict an explosion in processing power in the next decade, anything between 10- and 100-gig systems, with software to match. But that's not the end of the story. At the most recent Games Designers Conference, delighted fans and developers were able to get a taste of the future of gaming.

4d Rewrite all three extracts using a more formal style.

Reporting in speech

By the end of Part D you will be able to:
- refer to graphics and visual data
- refer to other sources in a presentation.

1 Referring to graphics and visual data

1a Work in pairs to discuss these questions about the costs and funding involved in space research and the development of technologies for space exploration.

1 Funding large-scale scientific programmes such as space research is extremely expensive. How important is it to get a return on investment for such programmes?

2 What are the possible benefits of space research for these institutions and stakeholders?
- governments
- universities
- businesses
- taxpayers

3 Is funding for space research justified during times of economic difficulty?

1b Look at the chart below, which shows how the budget for the European Space Agency is divided among projects over one year, and answer these questions.

1 What (approximately) is the total budget for all programmes?

2 Which programmes receive the most funding? Which the least?

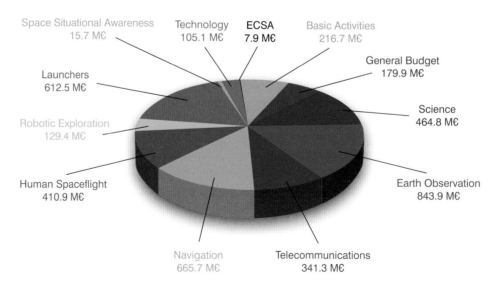

Figure 1: ESA budget by programme for 2011 (M€: million euros)

Source: European Space Agency http://www.esa.int/esaCP/index.html

2.10

1c Listen to an extract from a student's presentation, in which she discusses the above graphic, and answer these questions.

1 What background information does the student give about the chart?

2 Which parts of the chart does she highlight and discuss?

1d Work in pairs to discuss what words and phrases can be used for each of the functions in the right-hand column of this table. Then write your ideas in the left-hand column.

Words and phrases	Function
	Referring back to earlier parts of the presentation
	Referring to parts of the presentation which will come later
	Referring to a slide / to a visual display
	Referring to details within a slide / a visual

1e Listen again. Write notes below on the actual expressions the student uses for each of the functions in the above table.

Notes

1f Look at the transcript of the extract in **Appendix 3** and check your answers. Then add the phrases the student uses to the table in 1d.

1g Work in pairs. Imagine you are giving a presentation on early space exploration in the 1960s. Look at the summary on p.72 of planetary exploration conducted by the USA and the former USSR (modern-day Russia and the Commonwealth of Independent States). Then discuss these questions on how you could use this information to create a graphic for part of a presentation.

1 What conclusion(s) could you draw about early space exploration from this data?

2 Could you present the table on a slide as it is shown below? Why / why not?

3 How might you adapt the information to highlight your conclusions?

Table 2: Planetary exploration in the 1960s

Planetary Exploration				
SPACECRAFT	**MISSION**	**LAUNCH DATE**	**ARRIVAL DATE**	**REMARKS**
Venera 1 USSR	Venus probe	12 Feb., 1961	N/A	First Soviet planetary flight; launched from Sputnik 8. Radio contact was lost during USSR flight; spacecraft was not operating when it passed Venus.
Mariner 1 USA	Venus flyby	22 Jul., 1962	N/A	Destroyed shortly after launch when vehicle veered off course.
Sputnik 19 USSR	Venus probe	25 Aug., 1962	N/A	Unsuccessful Venus attempt.
Mariner 2 USA	Venus flyby	27 Aug., 1962	14 Dec., 1962	First successful planetary flyby. Provided instrument scanning data. Entered solar orbit.
Sputnik 20 USSR	Venus probe	1 Sep., 1962	N/A	Unsuccessful Venus attempt.
Sputnik 21 USSR	Venus probe	12 Sep., 1962	N/A	Unsuccessful Venus attempt.
Sputnik 22 USSR	Mars probe	24 Oct., 1962	N/A	Spacecraft and final rocket stage blew up when accelerated to escape velocity.
Mars 1 USSR	Mars probe	1 Nov., 1962	N/A	Contact was lost when the spacecraft antenna could no longer be pointed towards Earth.
Sputnik 24 USSR	Mars probe	4 Nov., 1962	N/A	Disintegrated during an attempt at Mars trajectory from Earth parking orbit.
Zond 1 USSR	Venus probe	2 Apr., 1964	N/A	Communications lost. Spacecraft went into solar orbit.
Mariner 3 USA	Mars flyby	5 Nov., 1964	N/A	Shroud failed to jettison properly; Sun and Canopus not acquired; spacecraft did not encounter Mars. Transmissions ceased nine hours after launch. Entered solar orbit.
Mariner 4 USA	Mars flyby	28 Nov., 1964	14 Jul., 1965	Provided first close-range images of Mars, confirming the existence of surface craters. Entered solar orbit.
Zond 2 USSR	Mars probe	30 Nov., 1964	N/A	Passed by Mars; failed to return data. Went into solar orbit.

Source: NASA http://www.nasa.gov

1h Use the space below to draw a plan for your graphic, including any text you will use.

Notes

1i Prepare notes on how you would present this slide. Make a note of language you could use from the table in 1d during your presentation.

1j Work in different pairs. Take turns to give your presentation of the 'slide' you drew in 1h.

2 Referring to other sources in a presentation (1)

2a Work in pairs to discuss these questions.

1 What do you understand by the term *tribal group*? What special characteristics do tribal groups have?

2 Have you ever met a member of a tribal group? Was this in your own country or abroad?

2.11

2b Listen and complete the extract from the lecture on isolated tribal societies from Part A.

> Around the world, there are perhaps 100 to 150 tribal communities which have resisted contact with the outside world, or indeed who have never had recorded contact with outsiders of any kind. These isolated societies often live in the heart of the world's densest jungles or remote islands, and have lived for centuries without contact with the world at large; they play no part in modern, globalized society. **1)** _____ the notoriously fierce Yanomami of Venezuela, who have welcomed outsiders in the past, but now resist contact, or the 100-strong group of islanders on Sentinel Island in the Indian Ocean, who have never been directly contacted by representatives of the modern world, and are openly hostile to outsiders attempting to land on the island. A helicopter which attempted to survey the island in the wake of the Indian Ocean tsunami of 2004 was met with a hail of arrows. **2)** _____ to this way of life; they maintain their freedom and cultural traditions, and have no apparent need of the trappings of modern life. **3)** _____ they also miss out on the obvious benefits that modernity can offer, such as education and advanced medical care.

2c Discuss the functions of the phrases you wrote in 2b.

2d Read the next part of the lecture and identify similar phrases.

> A new model of tourism is emerging which claims to reconcile these tribes with modern reality, allowing them to live their lives with dignity, while at the same time affording them meaningful and beneficial contact with the modern world; this model of tourism is commonly referred to as ethno-tourism – that is, tourism which is directly concerned with contact with exotic, isolated or simply different ethnic groups.

2e Work in pairs. Complete the text below with the phrases in the box.

> and others   claim that   heated debate   for instance   makes similar claims
>
> such as   there is evidence   undeniable

> There is 1)_____ about the impact of ethno-tourism on the tribal groups exposed to it. 2) _____, some anthropologists, 3) _____ James Morgan, who studied the result of contact between tourists and native groups in the Amazon basin, 4) _____ ethno-tourism has a profoundly negative effect on the groups exposed to it. Morgan, 5) _____, claim that it upsets the native groups' way of life, introducing culture shock, disease and previously unknown scourges such as alcoholism. The indigenous rights charity Survival International 6) _____ about the consequences of other tour groups' contact with natives around the world. While it is true – 7) _____ in fact – that contact between tribal groups and modern civilization has in the past all too often been negative, 8) _____ to suggest that, if properly managed, contact tourism can work to the advantage of local societies as well as the tourists themselves. There are, in fact, substantial benefits available to both sides of an ethno-tourism encounter.

2.12

2f Listen to the presentation and check your answers.

2g Work in pairs. Complete this table using the phrases you found in 2b, 2d and 2e. (Some could be used more than once.)

Referring to	Phrase
Specific examples	
Specific people's opinions	
General ideas	
General supporting information	

> **LESSON TASK** **3 Referring to other sources in a presentation (2)**

3a Discuss these topics in small groups.

1 Define the terms *immigration* and *emigration*.

2 Tell each other about any large immigrant groups in your community.

3 Tell each other about any problems you know which migrant communities face.

3b Listen to a lecture on the demographics of New Zealand's Pacific population and complete this extract.

2.13

First, then, I'd like to look at the general picture of the immigrant communities in New Zealand. Most of the recent migration to New Zealand has traditionally come from the Pacific, with areas such as the Cook Islands, Niue, Tokelau, Samoa, Tonga and Fiji being the main sources. People from the Cook Islands, Niue and Tokelau actually held New Zealand citizenship and therefore had unrestricted rights of entry and settlement in New Zealand. People from other Pacific nations, particularly Samoa, Tonga and Fiji, entered New Zealand in a variety of ways, including temporary permits, quota schemes and family reunification policies. **1)** _____ of small-scale illegal immigrant entry from these areas before the 1960s. So, by the 2006 Census, Pacific people in New Zealand numbered 266,000 and made up 6.9 per cent of the population. This is one of the highest proportions of immigrant population in the world and has been a **2)** _____, some parts of which I'd like to explore now.

This migration fuelled population growth in the 1960s and 1970s, so that by the time of the 1976 Census, there were almost 65,700 Pacific people living in New Zealand, which was about two per cent of the total population. An economic downturn in the 1970s resulted in a more restrictive immigration policy, but, even so, many Pacific people retained their rights of entry to New Zealand, so migration continued, albeit at lower levels. Since the mid-1990s, net migration gains from the Pacific have risen, averaging about 3,300 per year. The Pacific population in New Zealand has therefore continued to grow rapidly, and this has led **3)** _____ calling for tighter control over immigration. However, **4)** _____ suggests that it is actually not the recent immigration that has caused the overall rise in numbers, but the high rate of natural increase of these populations.

5) _____, as the graph shows, Samoans are by far the largest Pacific group in New Zealand, with over 130,000 people at the time of the 2006 Census. The Samoan population grew by 64,800 people – that's 98 per cent – between 1986 and 2006. This group in particular is a young population, with low rates of mortality and high rates of fertility. Pacific people are more likely than others to be in the age groups where most childbearing takes place and tend to have more children, with a fertility rate of three births per woman, compared with two births per woman for the total population. Because of their younger age structure, they also have a lower crude death rate of 3.2 deaths per 1,000 people per year, compared with 6.6 per 1,000 for the total population.

6) _____ provoked **7)** _____, with several political parties, such as Right New Zealand, calling for a rethink on immigration policy at the time. However, these views **8)** _____ from trade-union leaders and the immigrant communities themselves, who **9)** _____ without the immigrant population, the New Zealand economy would be unable to function properly in a number of key aspects. In May 2008, Dr Greg Clydesdale released a report, which saw Pacific Islanders as 'forming an underclass'. Pacific Islands community leaders **10)** _____, however, **11)** _____ the report, suggesting it was racially motivated.

Adapted from http://www.stats.govt.nz/browse_for_stats/people_and_communities/pacific_peoples/pacific-progress-demography/population-growth.aspx

3c Look at the graph on p.76, which shows the proportion of Pacific Islanders in New Zealand who speak English as their first language. What problems can you find with this graph? How could it be improved?

Pacific Peoples Speaking First Language and English
Usually resident population, 2001

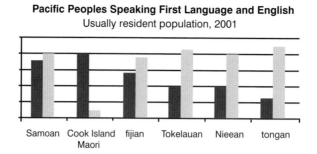

| Samoan | Cook Island Maori | fijian | Tokelauan | Nieean | tongan |

3d Work in pairs. Discuss how you would give feedback to the person who had produced the graph.

4 Review and extension

4a Read this paragraph and underline the phrases the writer uses to refer to different source material.

These claims of the positive benefits of cultured in-vitro meat have been challenged by economists, however. According to Keirle (2000, p.120), any environmental benefits from this method will be outweighed by the fact that it is economically uncompetitive when compared to traditional animal rearing. Farms are geared towards animal rearing, and the creation of enough of the right facilities to develop cultured meat would not only be enormously expensive in itself, but would mean the end of animal farming and consequent mass unemployment in that sector, with knock-on effects in the economy at large. Added to this is the problem of funding the further research needed to bring in-vitro meat to the point where it will be ready for commercial sale. Studies by Keirle (2000) as well as Monk (2000) estimate the investment of 3 to 4 billion dollars a year over the next decade in order to finish research and begin production of even a modest in-vitro meat operation. The view that cultured meat will be economically unviable is echoed by Aagard (2007, p.98), who believes that the consequences to the economy of the failure of the existing farming and associated industries will make cultured meat production entirely unviable, at least in the medium term.

4b Look at the information below on two island nations in the Indian Ocean: The Seychelles and The Maldives. In groups, discuss the similarities and differences between them, referring to the maps and table.

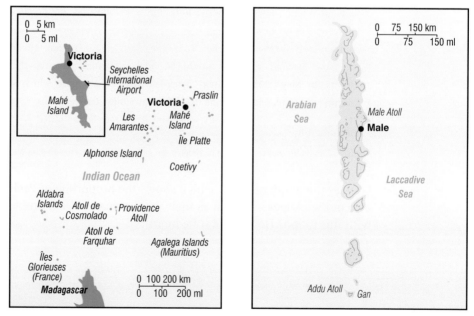

Country	Ethnicity	Languages	Urbanization
The Maldives	South Indian, Sinhalese, Arab	Maldivian Dhivehi (official) (dialect of Sinhala, script derived from Arabic), English spoken by most government officials	Urban population: 38% of total population (2008) Rate of urbanization: 5.3% Annual rate of change (2005–10 est.)
The Seychelles	Mixed French, African, Indian, Chinese, Arab	Creole 91.8%, English 4.9% (official), other 3.1%, unspecified 0.2% (2002 Census)	Urban population: 54% of total population (2008) Rate of urbanization: 1.4% Annual rate of change (2005–10 est.)

Source: https://www.cia.gov/library/publications/the-world-factbook/geos/se.html

4c Prepare a two-minute presentation providing information on the Indian Ocean islands. You can refer to texts in *Skills for Study Level 3*, the information above, your own general opinions or other sources you have researched.

4d Work in pairs and deliver your presentations. While one person is presenting to the class, the other should make a note in this table of the language and intonation used.

Did your partner use …	Yes	No	Example
examples?			
specific information or claims from others?			
general ideas and opinions?			
intonation for purpose and effect (i.e. fall–rise, rise tones)?			

Reporting in writing

By the end of Part E you will be able to:
- use *it* and *this* to link between sentences
- use *it* phrases to convey opinion.

1 Using *it* and *this* to link between sentences

1a Read this introduction to an article on in-vitro meat. Then work in pairs to discuss the function of *this* and *it* in the text.

> **'To what extent is in-vitro meat a suitable substitute for reared animal meat?'**
>
> A recent conference in Sweden optimistically concluded that in-vitro meat, a cultured meat grown artificially in a biotank, would be a viable commercial product within a decade (Van Der Zwan, 2009). The technology for developing **this** type of meat is sufficiently advanced that some test samples have already been created (though they are currently unfit for human consumption), and **it** seems that the prediction of commercial-grade in-vitro meat (hereafter IVM) within a decade is realistic. However, **it** is highly unlikely that **this** type of food will ever be a sufficient substitute for animal-reared meat, because of problems with nutritional content and public acceptance.

1b Read the next part of the article. Look at the words in bold and underline the parts of the text they refer to.

> The current aim of researchers involved in the development of IVM is to produce an artificial meat which is 'equal in protein and calorific content to animal-reared meats' (Naes, 2008, p.317). However, **this** ignores the fact that animal-reared meat is a much richer source of dietary nutrition than simple calories and protein. According to Sands (2007), all IVM samples so far created lack the range of nutrients which natural meats can provide, including irreplaceable vitamins and minerals.
>
> The true test of IVM's suitability as a commercial meat substitute is whether **it** sells well. Commercial IVM is unlikely to be readily adopted by consumers for two key reasons. Firstly, among the public at large there is a widespread dislike of highly artificial foodstuffs. **This** is evident in the suspicion with which genetically modified (GM) foodstuffs such as vegetables are treated. Sands (ibid) argues that **this** is more likely to be the case with animal flesh, as the thought of creating artificial flesh strikes many people as particularly revolting.

1c Work in pairs to discuss your answers.

1d Read the rest of the article on in-vitro meat, and complete it with either *it* or *this* in each gap. For some gaps, both may be possible.

> Nevertheless, for those in favour of IVM, Bell (2008) notes that a number of vegetarian and animal rights groups actively support its development, on the grounds that **1)** _____ allows for a rich source of protein that does not involve pain, cruelty or the death of an animal. According to Bell, **2)** _____ sentiment is likely to become more common as people recognize the quality of IVM, and will help people to overcome their initial caution about consuming **3)** _____ new food. Though vegetarian and animal

rights groups are undoubtedly correct in saying that IVM is an ethical alternative to reared animal meats, Bell's assertion that **4)** _____ will be enough to overcome widespread consumer suspicion about IVM seems doubtful.

Many people around the world (perhaps the majority) still refuse to eat GM food, despite the fact that **5)** _____ is routinely eaten by millions of Americans and there is no evidence, either scientific or anecdotal, to show that GM food is unhealthy. In light of **6)** _____ , I would argue that humans have a deep-seated horror at the idea of manipulating food, and **7)** _____ horror is unlikely to be shifted by ethical arguments or scientific evidence.

Furthermore, public acceptance of IVM is likely to be low because of the difficulty of producing a product which tastes sufficiently like meat. While IVM test samples have demonstrated that the muscle tissue can be grown, there is, to put it simply, more to the taste of meat than the tissue itself. For instance, many world cuisines rely on the use of animal bone marrow to enhance the flavour of the food. A related issue is the texture of the meat, which relies on muscular development through active movement of a healthy animal. **8)** _____ is unlikely that a tank-grown artificial meat would have a texture that many consumers would find satisfying due to the simple fact that the muscle was never stimulated by exercise.

In summary, IVM is a clear example of a product which, despite being technically possible, is extremely unlikely to enjoy commercial success. **9)** _____ is due to the fact that in-vitro meats are not a satisfactory nutritional substitute for existing natural meats. There seems to be a strong emotional attachment to the idea of natural meat, which any artificial substitute will struggle to overcome.

1e Write a short paragraph outlining your response to the text above. Do you think in-vitro meat represents a good alternative to usual farming methods? Use *it* and *this* in your writing to express this.

> *It* can be used to substitute another word. It can also be used as part of a fixed phrase.

1f Read these four extracts from different texts. Look at the words and phrases in bold and work in pairs to discuss how *it* is used in each case, as a substitute or part of a fixed phrase.

A

1) It is fair to say that modern business as we know **2) it** would be almost entirely impossible without the conveniences that email offers: swift communication with co-workers; the time and space to think through rapid communications in a way that is impossible in real time over the phone; the ability to send and receive large documents without the need for expensive and time-consuming printing or hand delivery. However, **3) it is clearly apparent that** email has also introduced a range of serious stress triggers into the workplace.

B

A far more troubling issue affecting personal privacy is the onward sale of one's personal data by the company to which **4) it** has been entrusted. This is a lucrative temptation for many businesses, which can profit by selling on bulk client data to marketing or other associated companies (Abbott, 2009, p.118). However, **5) it** is a practice which almost no organization is keen to admit to doing, and so data about the extent of this type of activity is scarce.

C

In a statement to the UK Food and Biotechnology Council, a leading in-vitro researcher noted that current methods of intensive farming of live animals for meat production clearly caused pain and distress for the animals involved. **6) It was further noted that** the culturing of completely artificial meat would be an effective answer to this, as the meat is grown without a nervous system, and therefore manufacturers are not faced with the ethical problem of causing pain (Chavez, 2009, p.108).

D

7) It has been shown that there is a lack of clarity in defining what is meant by 'formal' and 'informal', and whether these terms are used appropriately by course books. For example, course books often divide certain features of email into informal or formal (see Sections 2.2 and 2.3), but in this study a range of formality has often been distinguished in a single email.

1g Here are four further paragraphs, each containing a phrase with *it*. Identify them and decide which kind each one is.

1

Firstly, it is important to realize that gaming-as-educational-tool is not some possibility which lies only in the distant future; a number of popular educational games designed for students in the sciences and engineering already exist.

2

It is clear from the discussion outlined above that there are both potential benefits as well as philosophical and practical impediments to the production of in-vitro meat for human consumption.

3

Added to this is the problem of funding the further research needed to bring in-vitro meat to the point where it will be ready for commercial sale. Studies by Keirle (2000) as well as Monk (2000) estimate the investment of three to four billion dollars a year over the next decade in order to finish research and begin production of even a modest in-vitro meat operation.

4

The Online Privacy Commission has identified 30 cases in the last five years in which significant amounts of personal data were lost, either by accidental online transfer, or while being carried on a different media such as a USB file or even a laptop (OPC Privacy Report, 2009). It is impossible to determine what happened to this data after its loss, but the potential for abuse should not be underestimated.

1h Work in pairs to discuss your answers.

2 Using *it* phrases to convey opinion

It phrases can also give an idea of the writer's opinions.

2a Discuss if the two *its* in bold in this sentence refer to other words or phrases, or are part of fixed expressions.

*Though it is important to consider the cost, **it** is instructive to consider discoveries from space exploration and what technological advances **it** has enabled.*

2b Read this sentence, then answer the questions below.

It is instructive to consider discoveries from space exploration.

1 Which word class is *instructive*?

2 What is the writer's opinion about space exploration? Circle the best option.

   a It is important.   **b** It is useful.   **c** It is possible.

2c The words in the box can all be used in *it* phrases. Write them in the correct column of the table below.

apparent   astonishing   clear   doubtful   evident   important   interesting   likely
manifest   noteworthy   noticeable   obvious   plain   possible   probable   significant
surprising   unlikely

Importance	Attitude	Probability

2d These sentences from academic texts all contain *it* phrases. Separate them into two groups depending on the grammatical structure used after the *it* phrase.

1 It is impossible to predict which of these trends will continue over the next few years.

2 It is significant that the results were not consistent for all participants.

3 It is likely that this correlation will hold for all members of similar populations.

4 It is important to note that our conclusions are only tentative.

5 It is astonishing to find how far this idea has gained a foothold amongst sociologists.

6 It is clear that more research will be needed in this area.

7 It is evident that some of these results need re-examining.

8 It is obvious that these results have been influenced by changes in the atmosphere.

2e Write the two grammatical structures from 2d.

It phrase +

It phrase +

2f Which of the *it* structures in 2e cannot be followed by a verb?

2g Work in pairs. Give your opinions on these topics using some of the *it* phrases in this section. Use at least two different categories of *it* phrase for each topic.

video gaming	
in-vitro meat	
ethno-tourism	
space exploration	

> **LESSON TASK** | **3** **Identifying cohesion in texts**

3a Work in small groups. Discuss this essay title. Make notes summarizing the main points you discussed with your group.

Discuss the benefits and drawbacks of using in-vitro meat for human consumption.

Notes
Benefits
Drawbacks

3b Compare your notes with another student from the same group.

3c Work in pairs. Ignoring the gaps for now, read the extract on p.83 from the beginning of a student's essay on the same topic, then discuss these questions.

    1 Which benefit(s) and drawback(s) are mentioned?

    2 Do you believe the benefit(s) and drawback(s) mentioned are valid and relevant?

    3 What do you think is the author's attitude towards in-vitro meat for human consumption?

In-vitro cultured meat could soon be an everyday reality for millions of consumers. In-vitro meat is grown in a tank by culturing muscle cells from a living animal and enhancing them with artificial proteins. **1)** *This* is essentially the same technique as is already used for the production of yoghurt cultures. The ability to produce artificial meat in **2)** _____ way offers benefits to human health, the environment, and the welfare of animals currently bred for slaughter. However, **3)** _____ is a technology in its infancy, and though such meat has been successfully created in a number of experiments, no in-vitro meat is currently approved for human consumption. Important questions remain to be answered before **4)** _____ becomes a commonly accepted human food resource. **5)** _____ essay will consider arguments supporting the production of in-vitro meat, as well as those that maintain that such a method of meat production should not be pursued. The essay will conclude with **6)** _____ author's own view on the topic.

Experiments in the culturing of artificial meat have been continuing since the early 1990s, originally derived from NASA interest in a source of artificial protein for long-term space flights. In-vitro cultured meat offers a number of benefits: **7)** _____ is claimed that **8)** _____ is healthier than animal-grown meat, as food developers can control the nutritional content, in particular the fat content. A recent experiment (Olson, 2010, pp.43–44) showed that tank-grown in-vitro chicken was 80% leaner than its animal equivalent. Also, in-vitro meat is arguably kinder to animals. Scientists researching the possibilities of growing artificial meat find themselves in the rather odd position of being supported by vegetarian and vegan groups, as well as animal rights campaigners who normally focus on arguing against meat consumption. In a statement to the UK Food and Biotechnology Council, a leading in-vitro researcher noted that current methods of intensive farming of live animals for meat production clearly caused pain and distress for the animals involved. **9)** _____ was further noted that the culturing of completely artificial meat would be an effective answer to **10)** _____, as the meat is grown without a nervous system, and therefore manufacturers are not faced with the ethical problem of causing pain (Chavez, 2009, p.108).

3d Complete the text with either *it* or *this* in gaps 1–10. Sometimes either word may be possible. An example has been given to help you.

3e Check your answers with a partner. Then draw arrows from *this* or *it* to the part of the sentence they refer to. An example has been given to help you.

3f Read the extract below from another student's essay on the same topic. Look at the words in bold and answer these questions.

1   What do all these phrases have in common?

2   How do they help to create a more cohesive text?

A recent conference in Sweden optimistically concluded that **in-vitro meat, a cultured meat grown artificially** in a biotank, would be **a viable commercial product** within a decade (Van Der Zwan, 2009). The technology for developing **this type of meat** is sufficiently advanced that **some test samples** have already been created (though they are currently unfit for human consumption), and it seems that the prediction of **commercial-grade in-vitro meat** (hereafter **IVM**) within a decade is realistic. However, it is highly unlikely that **this type of food** will ever be a sufficient **substitute for animal-reared meat**, because of problems with nutritional content and public acceptance.

3g Read another extract from the same student's essay and underline all the words and phrases that refer to meat.

The current aim of researchers involved in the development of IVM is to produce an artificial meat which is 'equal in protein and calorific content to animal-reared meats' (Naes, 2008, p.317). However, this ignores the fact that animal-reared meat is a much richer source of dietary nutrition than simple calories and protein. According to Sands (2007), all IVM samples so far created lack the range of nutrients which natural meats can provide, including irreplaceable vitamins and minerals.

The true test of IVM's suitability as a commercial meat substitute is whether it sells well. Commercial IVM is unlikely to be readily adopted by consumers for two key reasons. Firstly, among the public at large there is a widespread dislike of highly artificial foodstuffs. This is evident in the suspicion with which genetically modified (GM) foodstuffs such as vegetables are treated. Sands (ibid) argues that this is more likely to be the case with animal flesh, as the thought of creating artificial flesh strikes many people as particularly revolting.

3h Write the synonyms for meat in the correct column of this table.

Natural	Artificial

3i As well as referring words and synonyms, texts are joined together by linking words. Complete the text below with the words in the box. In some cases, more than one answer is possible.

also   but   despite   even   however   however   indeed   no   only
order   such   this   that   well

Some questions remain, **1)**_____ , about the wisdom of pursuing research into in-vitro meat for human consumption. At a recent cross-disciplinary conference addressing issues raised by cultured meat production, leading experts in food anthropology, bioethics and tissue engineering argued that there are problems with public acceptance of this source of food (Lawton, 2009, p.21). Many people are likely to be 'extremely hostile to the idea of "lab-grown" meat' (Lawton, 2009, p.24), and it is likely that it would take a very long time for the food to gain widespread acceptance. This would mirror the situation with Genetically Modified (GM) vegetables, which remain deeply unpopular in many nations. Sheer disgust at the idea, **2)**_____ , is not the only problem affecting public acceptance. In **3)**_____ for public adoption of the new meat resource, developers must first create a meat which is not **4)**_____ essentially the same as animal meat on a molecular level, **5)**_____ looks, feels and, above all, tastes like the 'real thing' (Chavez, 2009, p.113). Without **6)**_____ , it is unlikely that in-vitro meat would ever overcome public prejudice against it, **7)**_____ matter how healthy, safe or ethically kind it was.

8)_____ the problem with consumer acceptance, researchers are confident that cultured meat will appear on supermarket shelves at some point in the near future. According to Monk (2000), **9)**_____ is due to external factors forcing the public to accept it, **10)**_____ perhaps in spite of themselves. Studies focusing on human population

11)_____ , overpopulation) and resource consumption have demonstrated that the adoption of artificial food technologies, including cultured meat and GM crops, will increasingly be seen as effective solutions to problems of world hunger and food security. One of the strongest claims in favour of pursuing the development of artificial meat is that it is better for the environment (Monk, 2000; Burwell, 2004a, 2004b; Wang, 2006). Cultured meat does not have any of the negative impacts associated with rearing cattle for slaughter, **12)**_____ as pollution from slurry and waste nitrates, as **13)**_____ as methane produced by the animals themselves. It **14)**_____ requires less water and makes land normally given over to rearing animals available for growing crops.

3j Match each of the words in the gaps in 3i with one of these functions.

a	addition	**e**	determiner
b	example	**f**	contrast
c	support	**g**	idiom
d	emphasis	**h**	cause

4 Review and extension

4a Complete this paragraph about in-vitro meat, making sure to use *it* and *this* appropriately, as well as any other linking devices which might be necessary.

> It is clear from the discussion outlined above that there are both potential benefits as well as philosophical and practical impediments to the production of in-vitro meat for human consumption. Benefits include …

4b Use opinion expressions from 2c to write sentences on these points:

1 The likelihood that space tourism will become widespread in the next 50 years.
2 The benefits of ethno-tourism.
3 Ethno-tourism in general.
4 The future of English as a global language.
5 Learning Chinese.
6 The Arctic environment.
7 The value of the Arctic for business.

Unit 3　The individual in society

Unit overview

Part	This part will help you to …	By improving your ability to …
A	Evaluate strong and speculative claims in speech	• identify the language of speculation • identify the language of past speculation • identify consonants and intrusive sounds.
B	Identify claims in a reading text	• understand the way claims are framed • evaluate claims in context.
C	Reconstruct notes and synthesize information	• reconstruct information from notes • write when synthesizing information from two or more sources.
D	Refer to other writers and research and present alternative arguments in presentations	• summarize key aspects of research in a presentation • present an oral argument with alternative viewpoints.
E	Paraphrase and punctuate academic texts	• identify and use substitution and ellipsis • identify and use different ways of paraphrasing.

Understanding spoken information

By the end of Part A you will be able to:

- identify the language of speculation
- identify the language of past speculation
- identify consonants and intrusive sounds.

1 Identifying the language of speculation

1a Write the parts of the 'identity' word family below.

Verb	Adjective(s)	Noun(s)
		identity

1b Below are some different aspects of identity. Work in pairs. Discuss which aspects of your identity you would be happy for the following people to have a record of.

partner   doctor   employer   immigration officer
mother   online friend   police officer   teacher

1 The colour of your skin	7 Your gender
2 Your DNA	8 The shape of your face
3 Your fingerprints	9 Your political beliefs
4 Your body weight	10 Your religion
5 The colour of your eyes	11 Your culture
6 Your nationality	12 Your emotions

1c Work in groups of three to four. Discuss which of the aspects of identity in 1b you think will be used in the future to identify people.

> In some academic situations it is acceptable for a speaker to speculate, or make guesses about things for which they have no evidence. Speculative claims can be described as *hedged* or *pure*.
>
> In hedged speculative claims the speaker acknowledges that there is uncertainty in their claim, and uses hedging and other expressions to help their audience judge the strength of the claim.
>
> In pure speculative claims the speaker makes strong claims, without supporting explanation or evidence, and does not use hedging.

1d Work in pairs. Discuss which type of speculation is considered more appropriate in academic contexts. Why?

1e Listen to two extracts from a lecture about identity and privacy in which the speaker makes speculative claims. Which claim is hedged and which one is pure speculation?

3.1

1f Work in pairs. You are going to listen to another extract from the lecture about identity. Before you listen, guess what the missing phrases might be using the examples given below.

are likely to see   is possible that we might   maybe   maybe some of you

may choose   perhaps one of the most   probably   seems likely that

some people choose   will probably become

All of us have at one time or another changed some aspect of our physical identity. We've all 1)_____ changed our hairstyles or clothing fashions at one point or another. 2)_____ you have had the experience of looking at an old passport photo of yourself and thinking that the person there is somehow no longer 'you' because your appearance has changed so much. But these days we can take physical changes much further, changing ourselves in ways that were impossible for earlier generations. 3)_____ have changed your eye colour with coloured contact lenses, for instance. 4)_____ plastic surgery in an effort to remake themselves, while others who are profoundly uncomfortable with their identity at birth 5)_____ a sex change – 6)_____ fundamental physical, and emotional, changes of the self. Technological advances, and also ideas within society about what is acceptable, offer us increasingly profound ways to change who we appear to be to the rest of the world. In the future we 7)_____ even more extreme forms of self-expression become normal. Plastic surgery 8)_____ more widespread. According to figures from consumer attitude surveys published by the Hughes Institute in the USA, the percentage of adults who would be prepared to have some form of plastic surgery has risen from 12% in 1995, to around 35% today, and it 9)_____ this trend towards seeing such surgery as a positive thing will continue ever upwards. As the technology develops, and such surgical procedures become cheaper, more socially acceptable and routine, it 10)_____ change between several radically different appearances throughout the course of our lives.

1g Listen to the lecture and check your answers.

1h Work in pairs. Read this transcript from later in the same lecture. Complete the transcript with phrases that you think are appropriate for each prediction.

For the police and border control agencies who rely on each of us having a constant physical identity, this 1)_____ present incredible challenges. DNA testing 2)_____ a more important method of identification than photographs, and so we 3)_____ see a greater social acceptance of the idea of national databases, where all citizens' DNA is stored. Passports 4)_____ include DNA samples rather than photographs. From the point of view of security, think of how this 5)_____ affect the use of Closed Circuit TV, or CCTV, cameras, that we see in buildings and all over our towns these days. Will these become useless if everyone is able to make radical changes to their appearance? Not so: in the future, CCTV 6)_____ be combined with sophisticated computer software which will recognize people caught on camera, not by their facial features, but by the unique way in which each of us walks, and extremely accurate measurements of things like height, shoulder width, the shape of your cheekbones, and so on. So, from a physical point of view, the future 7)_____ to change ourselves beyond all recognition, while at the same time 8)_____ scrutinized more closely than ever before by security technologies.

1i Listen to the extract and check your ideas.

1j Work in pairs. Compare your answers, then discuss these questions.

    1 Are the speaker's speculations hedged or pure?

    2 To what extent do you agree with the speculations? Give reasons.

> By using modal verbs or verb phrases it is possible to speculate about the likelihood of future events. This is usually done by replacing *will* in a future sentence with an appropriately cautious phrase.

1k Complete these claims with an appropriate word or phrase that represents your opinion about your society in the future.

    1 Plastic surgery _____ become more widespread.

    2 We _____ have several radically different appearances throughout the course of our lives.

    3 DNA testing _____ become a more important method of identification than photographs.

    4 Soon most of us _____ in societies where cash has been replaced by cards, electronic transfers and online shopping.

    5 Fewer people _____ willing to share information about themselves online. Social networking sites like Facebook, which are so popular now, _____ actually decline in popularity in the coming years.

1l Work in groups of three to four. Tell each other your opinion. Do you agree or disagree with each other? Explain your reasons and try to give evidence to support your claims.

2 Identifying the language of past speculation

> Speculation about events in the past is also acceptable when the speaker or writer is forced to guess about something for which no evidence is available.

2a Work in pairs. Use what you have learned about speculation already to decide which of these statements applies to more acceptable 'hedged' speculation about the past (H), and which describes less acceptable 'pure' speculation (P).

The speaker ...	H or P
1 bases their claims on untested assumptions.	
2 gives supporting reasons for their speculation.	
3 bases their claim on known facts.	
4 uses strong or extreme language to make the claim.	
5 uses hedging language.	
6 has not tried to find evidence before making their claim.	

2b In this statement, the speaker is speculating about an event in the past:

Many of us may have changed our hair, or even our eye colour.

Underline the part(s) of the sentence which show the speaker is leaving room for doubt about what has or has not happened in the past.

2c You are going to listen to a speaker discussing a social phenomenon in the USA. Before you listen, read this information about the topic and identify the phenomenon. Then speculate about possible explanations for the phenomenon with a partner.

> Researchers in the USA have noticed an unusual phenomenon in census data. The number of Americans between the ages of 25 and 29 identifying themselves as of Mexican heritage dropped in censuses between 1980 and the year 2000 (see Table 1 below). Researchers have confirmed that this drop is not related to mortality or emigration from the USA.
>
> **Table 1: Mexican Americans aged 25–29 years old, disappearing from census data, 1980–2000**
>
> | Year | 1980 | 1990 | 2000 |
> | --- | --- | --- | --- |
> | Male Mexican Americans | 262,940 | 246,710 | 203,719 |
> | Change on 1980 base | * | -6.2% | -22.5% |
> | Female Mexican Americans | 265,300 | 249,568 | 222,775 |
> | Change on 1980 base | * | -4.5% | -20.1% |
>
> Source: Alba & Islam, 2005

2d Listen to the lecture. What speculations does the speaker make about why the number of US citizens identifying themselves as of Mexican heritage has fallen?

3.4

2e Listen to extracts from the lecture, in which these claims are made. Make a note of the way that the speaker expresses each speculation.

2f Check your answers with a partner, then discuss whether each speculation is hedged or pure.

3.5

2g Listen to the speaker give another idea on the topic. Make a note of the claim that he makes.

3.6

2h Listen again. Decide if the claim is:

1 a strong claim (with reasons and supporting evidence)

2 hedged speculation (with supporting reasons and hedging)

3 pure speculation (without supporting reasons, evidence or hedging language).

2i Work with a partner. Make brief notes on the following topics. Then work in small groups. Use your notes to discuss the topics, using a variety of speculative language.

Life in the 1930s in your country	
Travelling abroad in the 19th century	
Writing academic essays before the invention of computers	

2j Work with a different partner. Write one speculative sentence for each of the topics in 2i.

2k Go back to your first partner. Check each other's sentences and answer the following questions:

   1 Is the speculation pure or hedged?

   2 To what extent do you agree with your partner's speculation?

3 Identifying consonants and intrusive sounds

3a Some of the sounds in this extract from a lecture have been underlined. Work with a partner. Say the single sounds to each other. Which of them are vowel sounds and which are consonant sounds?

> <u>Wh</u>at are the <u>c</u>omp<u>o</u>nents of <u>o</u>ne's 'identit<u>y</u>' as a h<u>u</u>man? We<u>ll</u> I suppose <u>m</u>ost people w<u>o</u>uld <u>a</u>ccept the ide<u>a</u> that we c<u>a</u>n <u>th</u>ink of identity in three ways. Firstly, there <u>are</u> the external, <u>p</u>hysical <u>ch</u>aracteristics, su<u>ch</u> as hei<u>gh</u>t and w<u>ei</u>ght ...

3b Work in groups of three or four. Practise saying these consonant sounds.

   • /t/ /d/

   • /p/ /b/

3c Say the sounds again thinking about how you are making the sound. What is the difference between the sounds in each pair?

3d Work in pairs. Match the sounds which can be paired, and write them in the table.

/dʒ/	/l/	/s/	/m/	/v/
/ʃ/	/ð/	/g/	/z/	/θ/
/ʒ/	/f/	/n/	/w/	/h/
/k/	/r/	/ŋ/	/j/	/tʃ/

Unvoiced	/p/	/t/
Voiced	/b/	/d/

3e Practise saying the sounds with a partner.

3.7

3f The following words have similar consonant sounds. Listen to the speaker. Tick (✓) the words you hear.

	A	(✓)	B	(✓)
1	pin		bin	
2	tear		dear	
3	tune		June	
4	crane		grain	
5	fast		vast	
6	think		sink	
7	they		say	
8	sue		zoo	
9	sheet		gîte	
10	came		cane	
11	pin		ping	
12	hurl		earl	
13	light		right	
14	what		yacht	

3g Check your answers with a partner.

3h Work in pairs. Practise saying some of the words. See if your partner can identify them correctly.

3i Read this extract from a lecture on identity. Underline the first consonant sound in the stressed syllables in bold. The first two have been underlined as examples.

> <u>Hu</u>mans are e<u>ss</u>entially like **oth**er living creatures: we are made of **cells**, we have a **sim**ilar **chem**ical composition, we have a system of **org**ans inside our **bod**ies, **and** we re**pro**duce. We **al**so carry basic ge**net**ic infor**ma**tion inside our **bod**ies. But **one** of the things that **mak**es us dis**tinct** from **oth**er animals is that **each** of us has a **clear** sense of our **own**, **ind**ividual, i**den**tity.

3j Identify the consonant sounds at the beginning of the stressed syllables. Write words from the text next to the correct sounds. Then add one more word of your own choosing.

/h/ humans	/s/ essentially	/ð/	/k/	/g/
/b/	/r/	/l/	/n/	/m/
/z/	/t/	/tʃ/	/d/	/w/

3k Work in pairs. Practise saying the individual words. Then listen to the extract from 3i. Practise saying it with a partner.

3.8

In rapid speech, native speakers often add *intrusive sounds* between words.

Examples
1 *One of the things that makes us distinct from other /**r**/animals …*
2 *We /**j**/are made of cells …*
3 *From the point of view of governments, the police, companies and so/**w**/ on …*

3l Match each of these intrusive sounds with one of the examples in **bold** above.

a All of us have at one time <u>or an</u>other …

b … in which each of us walks, and extremely accurate measurements of things like height, shoulder width, the shape of your cheekbones and <u>so on</u>.

c … the future will <u>see us</u> able to change ourselves beyond all recognition …

3m Work in pairs. Discuss the situations in which each intrusive sound is used.

3n Listen to the speaker and complete the extract. What intrusive sounds are used?

3.9

What are the components of one's 'identity' as a human? Well I suppose most people would accept **1)**_____ that we can think of identity in three ways. Firstly, **2)**_____ the external, physical characteristics, such as height and weight; the **3)**_____ **4)**_____ _____, your hair and skin; as well as any particular physical characteristics which mark **5)** _____ different **6)**_____ _____ – a bigger than average nose, maybe, **7)**_____ opposed to straight hair. These are the physical characteristics that, in the popular view, **8)**_____ stuck with throughout your life.

➤ LESSON TASK | 4 Speculating on a topic

4a You are going to listen to a lecture on biometrics. Work in pairs. Before you listen, discuss these questions.

1 What does the word 'biometrics' mean?

2 Have you ever been asked to give biometric information?

4b The following text is from a lecture on biometrics. With a partner, discuss what words might fill the gaps, using speculative language.

> So what is 'biometrics'? Perhaps the word is unfamiliar to some of you, but I am **1)**_____ that all of you have had experience of giving, or using, biometric data of some sort. The clue is in the Greek origin of the word; 'bio', meaning **2)**_____, and 'metric', meaning **3)**_____. So biometrics is the **4)**_____, or recording, of data about our unique physical characteristics. Your passport photo is a piece of biometric data, recording the unique shape of your **5)** _____. If you have ever been asked to give a fingerprint, that is also biometric information – the unique pattern on each of our fingertips can be measured, recorded, and used to identify us. A **6)**_____, too, is a kind of biometric measurement. Each of us writes our signature in a particular manner, a certain pattern in the movements of our **7)**_____ and fingers which, it is hoped, uniquely identifies us. So biometrics is the use of unique **8)**_____ to identify or recognize individuals. These can be physiological – that is, physical identifiers, such as fingerprints or face shape – or behavioural identifiers, such as the way in which you use a pen to sign your name.

3.10

4c Listen to the extract. Check your answers.

4d Work in small groups. Complete these activities regarding the development of biometric systems.

1 List four possible purposes of using biometric data to identify people.

2 Speculate on the kind of traditional identification 'systems' that could be replaced by more modern biometric ID systems.

3 Discuss the possible disadvantages of using photographs and signatures for identification purposes.

4 Generally, two main types of biometric data are given – physiological and behavioural. Classify these possible sources of biometric identification into the two categories. Write your answers in the table on p.95.

> body odour analysis   breath analysis   DNA   facial structure
> fingerprints   gait measurement[1]   hair colour
> hand geometry   height   iris recognition   keystroke dynamics[2]
> personal vocabulary analysis   reading speed
> retina blood vessel recognition   shoe size   signature scans
> timing of 100 metres run   typing speed   voice recognition

[1] the way you walk   [2] how you use a keyboard

Physiological	Behavioural

5 Which ones would make effective biometric identification measures? Why / why not? Discuss which four might be the most effective for each type.

3.11

4e Listen to the next extract from the lecture and check your predictions and speculations in 4d.

4f Work in pairs. Speculate about what factors need to be considered to make a biometric identification system effective and workable.

Notes
be fast / give instant decisions

3.12

4g Listen to the next extract. See if your ideas are mentioned. Note down any other factors you didn't think of.

4h Complete these sentences with an appropriate verb and a suitable speculation phrase (including positive or negative modals) showing your position on these areas of biometrics.

Example

*By 2015, fingerprint analysis keys **are highly likely to be used** for starting personal computers.*

1 By 2030, palm prints _____ house doors.

2 By 2040, all passports _____ biometric data stored inside.

3 In ten years' time, eye scans _____ shopping in supermarkets.

4 Students _____ voice recognition to write essays.

5 In the next five years, cars _____ your breath before starting.

6 There _____ less crime than there is now.

7 In the future, the use of biometric data _____ the use of passports redundant.

4i Work in pairs. Discuss whether you agree or disagree with each other's opinions.

5 Review and extension

3.13

5a Listen to the speaker and tick (✓) the words you hear. If there are any words you don't know, check their meaning in a dictionary.

	A		B	
1	bear		pear	
2	dawn		torn	
3	tune		June	
4	crate		grate	
5	vet		fête	
6	these		seize	
7	thank		sank	
8	sane		same	
9	sing		sin	
10	haul		all	
11	long		wrong	
12	wet		yet	

5b Choose one of the words in italics and then complete the sentence with an appropriate past modal or other speculative language.

1 In the past, it _____ *easier / harder* to write essays in higher education without computers.

2 20 years ago, it _____ *easier / harder* to travel for people from my country.

3 There _____ *less / more* crime than today due to the introduction of CCTV.

4 Life _____ *less / more* private in the past without technological surveillance.

5c Circle the correct intrusive sound between the two underlined words.

1 /w/ /j/ Technological advances, and <u>also ideas</u> within society about what is acceptable …

2 /r/ /j/ In the future <u>we are</u> likely to see …

3 /j/ /w/ For the police and border control agencies who <u>rely on</u> each of us having a constant physical identity …

4 /w/ /r/ … all <u>over our</u> towns these days …

5d Read the passage below and mark where intrusive sounds would probably go in natural speech.

> You have an identity at work, we can say, if you love your job enough that you identify with your job or company. But do you behave in the same way when you are at home with your family? Are you, literally, the same person? When, at the weekend, you throw off your work identity and go to meet some friends, are you the same person then? And when in the evening you change your hairstyle and clothes and go and dance at a nightclub, or go to pray at a place of worship? When you are angry, are you the same person as when you are calm? If we could track the way you behave in cyberspace – your web-surfing habits, or maybe an online game which you are involved in, and in which you assume a completely different character – would we recognize you as the same person that we see in real life?

Understanding written information

By the end of Part B you will be able to:
- understand the way claims are framed
- evaluate claims in context.

1 Understanding the way claims are framed

1a Read these texts. Which one is purely factual and which contains opinions or claims?

A

Identity fraud may be defined as the practice of using personal information to access bank details and carry out transactions or business without the permission of the individual. Identity fraud is considered to be unlawful. Identity fraud usually involves stolen or forged documents, such as a passport or a driving licence. As well as identity fraud, there is also the practice of identity theft – using someone's personal details to obtain goods, services or information. In the UK, identity fraud affected 89,000 individuals and was thought to cost the economy £1.2 billion in 2008 alone.

B

Identity fraud has been considered as the UK's fastest-growing crime for the last few years. It is estimated to cost the UK economy at least £1.3 billion each year according to UK government statistics (Cabinet Office, 2008). There seems to be a general agreement among crime analysts that this is one of the most difficult frauds to combat. Professor Davies pointed out that this is largely because, on average, it takes up to 14 months for victims to realize that their details have been stolen (Davies, 2009, p.63). It has been argued that the best solution is for individuals to take steps to avoid becoming a victim in the first place. However, critics have questioned this position, arguing that the banking industry needs to do more to combat the crime.

> Although it is essential that claims are supported by factual information, a purely descriptive text is usually unacceptable at higher education level. Most texts need to contain a mixture of claims and supporting reasons and evidence.

1b Underline the claims in Text B.

1c Add the phrases used to introduce those claims to this table.

	Making claims
Referring to the claims of others	Many researchers **have suggested that** ... Professor Jones **subscribes to the view that** ... 1 ... has been considered as ... 2 3
Indicating that a claim seems valid or pertinent	He **makes a valid point when he argues that** ...

Indicating agreement on a claim	**There is some common ground on** the origins of this problem. Many experts **concur that** … 4
Indicating disagreement about a claim	Others **have challenged** this view. Many **have taken issue with** this suggestion. 5

1d Complete these claims with an appropriate word or phrase from 1c.

    a Although there has been considerable support for the use of CCTV cameras in crime prevention, many others _____ this view, arguing that the money invested would be better spent on other forms of policing.

    b Dr Jones _____ when he argues that the role of CCTV in preventing crime is difficult to measure.

    c Many experts would probably _____ that the benefits of further expansion of CCTV are doubtful.

    d Recent research _____ that the number of CCTV cameras that are fully operational may be considerably lower than the 4.2 million figure.

2 Evaluating claims in context

2a Work in pairs. Discuss these questions.

    1 Which do you think is a more effective tool for fighting crime: DNA databases or ID cards?

    2 Do you know of any cases where DNA evidence has been used to help solve a particular crime?

2b This text compares DNA databases and the introduction of ID cards which contain biometric information. Read it quickly. Identify why the writer doesn't support the use of biometric ID cards.

Why I am against biometric ID cards

A Can you support Britain's current DNA database, yet oppose plans for biometric ID cards? It's a difficult issue.

B The past week has seen three men convicted of murder, and all three were either convicted or suspected of multiple killings. In two cases, DNA evidence proved vital: their DNA had been acquired through the current procedure whereby if someone is arrested, his or her DNA is taken and recorded (as a set of 20 numbers) on the national database. Previous crimes where DNA has been recovered but no other match found are then checked against new entries.

C It is beyond argument that the database is a fantastic tool for solving crime. I think it is also right that arrest should be the trigger for taking a sample, since it's logical that someone who has committed a serious crime will probably commit smaller ones too. For this reason I'm against the case currently being brought by two people who were arrested but not charged and want their DNA details removed from the database. Arrest may be a weak indicator, but it's still an indicator.

D Equally, I'm against widening DNA collection to the whole population. The reasons were elegantly spelt out in *The Guardian* on Thursday by Professor Allan Jamieson: 'The larger [the database] becomes, the greater the chance is of a fortuitous "hit", false conviction, and unnecessary stress on individuals and resource deployment by the police.' And since the Home Office minister Tony McNulty agrees, I don't think there's much risk of the DNA database encompassing all of us.

E OK, but what about biometrics – iris scans, fingerprints, facial recognition – for ID cards? After all, consider benefit fraud, which is estimated to have cost the taxpayer £2.5bn in 2006/7. In one article, a minister for the Department for Work and Pensions said that 'the introduction of identity verification services, to be provided by the Identity and Passport Service as part of the National Identity Card scheme, will have a significant impact on the ability of fraudsters to make claims for social security benefits using more than one identity.' However, in the same article, the minister admitted that no estimate has been made of the value of fraudulent claims which could be detected annually simply by keeping accurate records of addresses. Clearly, it's a case of selective information.

F More to the point, an ID card would be used to prevent benefit fraud – not to prove who committed the crime after the fact. If you had to give an iris scan when making each benefit application, that would make multiple fraudulent applications harder. But the fact that one woman could claim for an amazing 18 non-existent children doesn't suggest that the system for detecting unusual claims is very robust at the moment. Introducing iris scans and fingerprinting all parents and children before they can get child benefit would create a ludicrous, expensive system that could still be gamed.

G It is that presumption of guilt, though – the thinking that you're only out to cheat the system – that seems so wrong about the national biometric database. Leave aside the issue of how secure it might be. Nobody can change your biometrics, just as they can't change your DNA. The key is that it assumes you're guilty. And that's what's so unacceptable.

H The point about the DNA database is that it only comes into play after a crime has been committed, and when someone is suspected of it. At that point, you become a suspect in all unsolved crimes with DNA evidence. But in claiming benefit, or trying to board an aeroplane, we're not committing a crime. And in a society that likes to call itself 'free', the presumption of innocence is surely the most important title we can give everyone, even if it is disappointed by fraudsters and killers. It has been the bedrock of our legal system for centuries. And that, in short, is why I support the DNA database, even for suspected criminals, but do not support a nationwide biometric database. Innocent unless proven guilty is an important freedom. Let's stick with it.

Adapted from: Arthur, C. (2008, February 29). Why I am against biometric ID cards. *The Guardian*. Retrieved from: http://www.guardian.co.uk/technology/2008/feb/29/dna.database

2c Underline places where the writer:

a uses a persuasive style of writing **c** gives supporting evidence

b gives their own opinions **d** draws conclusions.

2d Look at these persuasive features of writing in the text (1–6). Add them to the table on p.101.

1 *It is beyond argument that* the database is a fantastic tool for solving crime.

2 I think it is also right that arrest should be the trigger for taking a sample, *since it's logical that* someone who commits a serious crime will probably commit smaller ones too.

3 Arrest *may be a weak indicator, but it's still an indicator*.

4 The reasons were *elegantly spelt out* in *The Guardian* on Thursday …

5 The introduction of identity verification services ... will have *a significant impact on* the ability of fraudsters to make claims for social security benefits using more than one identity.

6 *It has been the bedrock of our legal system for centuries*.

Function	Examples of typical language used
Claiming that your own position is particularly strong	**Any other conclusion would**, I suggest, **be** illogical. a It is beyond argument that … b c
Suggesting a lack of better alternatives	**In the absence of** any concluding evidence, countries should not introduce this policy. d
Making non-specific claims	**The effect of** a slight rise in the earth's temperature **would be** huge. e
Appealing to emotions or a sense of tradition	**It is the only** moral option **available** in a civilized society. f
Discrediting an opposing argument	**Much of the criticism comes from** writers with their own agenda.

2e Work in pairs. Discuss how useful the text in 2c would be as support in an academic essay on the following topic: 'Outline the arguments for and against introducing a biometric ID card system.' Would you use it? Why / why not? How could you make use of it?

> **LESSON TASK**   **3 Identifying and assessing claims**

3a Work in small groups. Make a list of the individual rights you think people under the age of 16 should have.

Example

They should have the right to attend school.

Rights people under the age of 16 should have

3b Work in small groups. Read these essay titles. Discuss your opinions about them.

Essay titles	Text(s) A–D
1 The collection of data on children needs to be more strongly regulated than that on adults. Discuss.	
2 To what extent do children hold the same set of individual rights as adults?	
3 Discuss the extent to which child protection measures should override the individual rights of a child.	

3c Read these four texts (A, B, C and D) quickly and decide which ones you would use to support your writing in one of the essays above. Write your answers in the right-hand column of the table in 3b.

A Extract on the rights of children under the UN Charter

The rights of children are seen as non-negotiable and set a minimum standard of rights and freedoms that should be provided by governments. In 1989 it was agreed by the UN Charter that children under the age of 18 have special needs and rights to protections that are distinct from those over the age of 18. The Charter was based on the four principles of protecting a child from discrimination, allowing a child to develop to his or her fullest potential, the right to survival and self development, and a respect for the views of children. The Charter sets standards in healthcare, education, rights for protection if the child has to work, rights to access legal and social services, and protection from the worst forms of abuse and exploitation.

Governments who sign up to the Charter are obliged to accept the principles and provide for those children living within their territories.

Source: UNICEF, 2011

B Extract on children's information held in databases

An independent research report has highlighted concerns over the use of children's personal information being stored in databases. Information about children and those associated with them is collected with good motives. We all want to protect children from abuse or other forms of harm and allow them to achieve their full potential with the best possible healthcare, education, and social and emotional development. There is also a strong desire to stop children from drifting into a life of crime and anti-social behaviour.

However, how any information can best be used to ensure that this happens is a source of considerably more controversy. European law on data protection currently makes no distinction between the data of an adult and that of a child. Many of the issues that arise around the handling of data held on children call for delicate judgements to be made.

Records currently held include: extensive factual records and educational records of every child in state education in the UK; records of all children; specific databases for children receiving social care and counselling, which contain very detailed records of the child and their family; profiles of young offenders for the purpose of rehabilitating them; similar profiles of children who have not yet committed an offence but are identified as being at risk of committing a criminal offence; and detailed records of any children registered as unaccompanied asylum seekers, or those who have appeared in homeless records.

More decisions need to be taken on the extent and range of data that may be held on individual children by official bodies and how this information is to be shared with other organizations.

Greater clarity about the key issues of data protection is needed. Clarity about the purposes, rationales and legal authority are important considerations in deciding what is and is not acceptable. Also, it is essential that agreement is reached between the official bodies involved to ensure that they get the balance right, not least to ensure public trust and confidence in what they do.

The current system, with a lack of clarity and specific guidance on such issues, leaves those involved in data collection in a weak position.

Source: UK Information Commissioner's Office, 2011

C Extract on the growing trend of identity theft of minors in the US

Since the 1980s, children in the US have been issued with Social Security Numbers (SSN) from birth. However, by law, they cannot be offered credit using their SSN as identification until the age of 18. A child's SSN is therefore dormant for credit purposes for 18 years. Criminal organizations have found ways to take advantage of these dormant SSNs, using them to create credit histories for those who have poor credit rating, are illegal immigrants or have other criminal intent. Because credit providers are unable to verify the age of the holder of the SSN, many children have had their identity stolen without them ever knowing it. The crime of identity theft is rarely spotted until the child turns 18.

The Identity Theft Research Bureau has proposed the creation of a Minors 17-10 Database to combat this problem. The list would register all children from birth until they reach the age of 17 years and 10 months. The Social Security Authority would extract the name, date of birth and SSN number, and would then be able to advise credit providers if the number they have belongs to a minor.

Source: US Identity Theft Resource Center, 2010

D Extract from an editorial on the decision to remove one child database

As an organization in daily contact with children across the country, many of whom desperately need better co-ordinated and better quality universal services, the decision to remove the Contact Point database, originally set up to improve outcomes for children, has hindered the facilitation of communication between the various agencies working with children and young people.

Contact Point had the potential to significantly enhance professional responses to children in need of help. It would allow practitioners to quickly assess who else had been working with the same child as themselves, and how they could contact them. Time and again, when high profile cases of child deaths have been reviewed, lack of communication between the various agencies is identified as a significant contributing factor to the failure of social services to act in the interests of the most vulnerable children. The Contact Point database was set up in response to the findings of Lord Laming in his review of the death of eight year old Victoria Climbie at the hands of her aunt and her aunt's boyfriend.

While it is essential that we do not impinge on children's civil liberties, child protection should come before concerns about governments having too great an access to an individual's data. Concerns over the checking of those allowed to see the database for criminal records needs to be reviewed again, as does the issue of data protection rights. But while families are able to avoid scrutiny by moving frequently from one town to another, a national database is the only form of protection for extremely vulnerable children. Public bodies have an obligation to safeguard the human rights of children above all other issues.

Source: Penny Nicholls, Director of the Children's Society, (*Guardian*, 2010)

3d Choose one of the essay questions in 3b. Make notes on the texts which are relevant to that question. Use the Cornell note-taking system.

    1 Make notes in the right-hand column on the main claims in the text, and any factual support that is offered.

    2 Identify the conclusions that the different writers draw.

    3 Add your comments on the validity of the claims in the left-hand column.

    4 Compare and discuss your notes.

3e Use your notes to match the ideas below with the texts where these claims are made.

    1 There may be data collected on children who have no criminal record, but are deemed likely to commit crime in the future.

    2 It is a requirement of modern nation states that they respect and promote the rights of children.

    3 Weaknesses in the system of issuing a particular kind of identity have made children vulnerable to becoming the victims of crime.

    4 There are no special regulations regarding the protection of children's personal information.

    5 Those who gather information on children have good intentions.

    6 The advantage of one database was to improve communication between people working to safeguard children.

    7 There are currently not enough guidelines on controlling access to child databases.

    8 Some aspects of human rights are unique to children.

3f Work in pairs. Decide which claims would help you to answer the first essay question in 3b.

3g Have you changed your position? Report back on your discussions to the others in the class.

4 Review and extension

4a Match a word or phrase on the left (1–5) with a definition on the right (a–e).

1 correlation	a agree
2 statistically significant	b disagree with
3 correspond to	c found to be important by using a mathematical formula
4 concur	d be the same or very similar
5 take issue with	e a relationship or connection between two things

4b Look at the sentences below. Find a more appropriate way to express these views using the words or phrases in 4a.

1 I think that the researchers have found something important.

_____

2 Obviously, poverty and bad health are the same thing.

_____

3 Professor Brown thought the researchers had got it all wrong.

_____

4 Nobody knows if more children are harmed because we keep databases.

_____

5 Dr Clarke was right when he intelligently put forward his criticism of these views.

_____

Investigating

By the end of Part C you will be able to:

- reconstruct information from notes
- write when synthesizing information from two or more sources.

1 Reconstructing information from notes

1a Look at these notes and the extract from a report below, which has been reconstructed from the notes. In the extract, underline all the words or phrases the writer has used directly from the notes.

Welsh, B., and Farrington, D. (2007). Closed-circuit Television Surveillance. In Welsh, B. and Farrington, D. (Eds.), Preventing Crime : What works for children, offenders, victims and places (pp. 193-208). NY : Springer Science + Business Media

Alternative measures ⟶ security paint
Lighting

How cost-effective
is CCTV ⟶ cutting back foliage
by comparison? (p.206) police patrols

Aim of CCTV ⟶ To prevent
1) personal crime p.193
"Tremendous growth" 2) property crime p.193
of CCTV in UK. (p.194) 3) Aid crime detection p.194
1999-2001 £ 170 mill. 4) Increase public p.194
in UK. confidence

Problems

"Much debate" about effectiveness of CCTV. (p.195)
Many studies of benefit are not conclusive.
Evaluates findings from 22 studies.
1) city centre + public housing → "mixed results"
(p.198)
2) public transport "conflicting evidence" (p.202)
3) car parks — most positive effects
Overall vehicle crime ↓ 28% !
violent crime ↓ 3%
Effect is "small but significant" (p.203)
However, positive effects may not continue long after
first installation (p.206)
public support + privacy

UK — public support for CCTV is high (p.205)
USA — low public support — fear 'Big Brother'
and invasion of privacy (p.205)

The UK has seen a 'tremendous growth' in the use of CCTV, with over £170 million being spent on installation from 1999–2001 (Welsh & Farrington, 2007) and it is important to ask whether this has been an effective use of money. CCTV can benefit the fight against crime in a number of different ways. Firstly, Welsh and Farrington (ibid) argue that CCTV helps prevent both personal crime (such as mugging and rape) and property crime (e.g. shoplifting, the theft and damage of cars and buildings, and burglary). Secondly, once a crime has been committed, CCTV can help detection rates by providing sightings of those responsible. Finally, CCTV appears to increase public confidence in the authorities, that crime is being taken seriously (Welsh & Farrington, 2007). However, in terms of cost-effectiveness, there may be other strategies (e.g. security paint, better lighting in unlit areas and increased police presence) that could give the same benefits as CCTV, but at a lower economic cost.

1b Look at the words or phrases you have not underlined. Find examples of the language features listed in the table.

Language features	Example(s)
Articles and determiners	
Hedging language	
Linking words and phrases	
Noun phrases	
Reporting verbs	
Words and phrases for introducing examples	

> Note making involves breaking down source texts and recording only the most relevant and significant information. When the time comes to produce an essay, these notes are then reconstructed using the writer's own words to generate the new, original text.

1c Discuss which of these things the writer of the report has done when reconstructing the notes. Write (T) true or (F) false.

The writer has:	True (T)	False (F)
A used the note information to support a main point (topic sentence).		
B re-ordered information from the notes.		
C put pieces of information together into longer units (using clauses and link words).		
D given examples to make some terms clearer to the reader.		
E used all the words or phrases taken as notes.		
F indicated to the reader how sure or unsure the writer is over some of the evidence used.		
G changed some of the word forms from the notes.		

1d Look at the two sets of notes about some of the problems of using CCTV in **Appendix 4**. Reconstruct these notes to produce a short paragraph about problems connected with CCTV.

2 Writing when synthesizing information from two or more sources

Information from two or more sources can be used by a writer in a process known as synthesis. By synthesizing information, the writer compares and contrasts the information in each source to help develop and express their own, original, position on a topic.

2a Work in pairs. Tell each other what you understand by the term 'identity theft'.

2b Decide whether you think these pieces of information about identity theft are true (T) or false (F).

	True (T)	False (F)
A Some six million people in the UK claim to have been victims of identity theft.		
B It could take you anytime from six months to two years to recover from being a victim of identity theft.		
C Some estimates put the cost of identity theft in the UK at £1.7 billion per year.		
D In the world, a crime involving identity theft takes place approximately every eight seconds.		
E Identity theft is one of the fastest-growing crimes in the UK, increasing at 500% year on year.		
F Around 18 million households in the UK regularly throw away sensitive financial documents such as bank statements without shredding them.		
G People who earn over £60,000 annually are three times more likely to be victims of identity theft.		
H People aged 31 to 40 are the most likely to be repeat victims of identity theft.		

2c Work in small groups. Discuss your opinions on these questions.

1   How serious is identity theft?

2   What are the main causes and effects of identity theft?

2d Read the extract on p.109 from a report on identity theft in the UK. Does this text support or conflict with the information in 2b?

Recent research relating to the risks of identity theft has established that this is perhaps one of the fastest growing and most serious crimes facing consumers in the UK, with far-reaching effects on victims. According to Davis (2007), if you are a young, male professional living in the London area then you are at most risk of becoming a victim of identity fraud. Likewise, research by Benson and Foulden (2008) shows that those in the younger age groups (aged 31 to 40) are more liable to become victims and that this is more likely of males than females. Other research of the most likely victims (Henson, 2006; Francis, 2007) similarly regards this group as being the most susceptible to identity theft and notes that the chances of being a victim of identity theft are highest for those who live in London and the south-east of the UK, although Grebe and Holden (2007) claim that it is in regional cities such as Manchester and Nottingham, rather than London, that victims are most likely. Both Henson (2006) and Davis (2007) suggest that it can take more than 300 hours for victims to be able to clear their names with credit companies and set up new bank accounts after identity theft.

2e The report writer has used a number of different sources as support and has synthesized the information from these different sources. Look at the extract again and decide what the point is that is being discussed. Then decide whether the sources highlight an agreement or a disagreement regarding that point. Complete the rest of the table.

Point made by report writer	Sources used	Source agreement / disagreement
Typical victim of identity theft likely to be young males	Davis (2007) Benson and Foulden (2008)	Agree
Where a typical victim comes from		
Amount of time needed for victims to clear their name		

2f Find three words or phrases in the extract that the writer uses to show **agreement** between the sources.

2g Look at this sentence from the extract. Which of the words from 2f could go in the gap?

_____ research by Benson and Foulden (2008) shows that those in the younger age groups (aged 31 to 40) are more liable to become victims and that this is more likely of males than females.

2h Find two other places for the same words to go in the extract in 2g.

2i Here are some other ways you can show agreement when synthesizing information from different sources. Underline any words or phrases that indicate agreement.

1 With respect to the importance of long-term effects, Creed (2007) and Farndale (2009) are in agreement.

2 Creed (2007) and Farndale (2009) take a similar position with regard to the importance of long-term effects.

3 As far as the importance of long-term effects is concerned, Creed (2007) and Farndale (2009) have corresponding views.

4 Similar views regarding the importance of long-term effects are held by Creed (2007) and Farndale (2009).

2j When synthesizing information, it is also often necessary to outline to the reader the area of agreement. Using the same sentences, underline the phrases in 2i which show the reader the area of agreement. An example has been given to help you.

Example

With respect to the importance of long-term effects, Creed (2007) and Farndale (2009) are in agreement.

2k Read another extract from a report on identity theft in the UK. Complete the table below in the same way as in 2e.

> Although the costs of identity fraud are enormous to individuals, financial institutions and businesses, it is not always easy to calculate what these might be. According to Benson and Foulden (2008), the total cost to individual victims in the UK was approximately £7.1 million for 2007, with an average loss of £480, whereas Lamont (2009, 45) claims that the amount for the same year was 'in excess of £8.5 million with an average loss of nearer £600'. Henson (2006) estimated that the current average loss to banks, credit card firms, insurers and other businesses affected by identity theft in the UK is between £1.5 billion and £1.7 billion, while Davis (2005) puts the figure at £1.4 billion. On the other hand, Medway (2009) puts the figure much higher at more than £2.8 billion, although this figure includes losses which go unreported, which are apparently as high as 30 per cent.

Point made by report writer	Sources used	Source agreement / disagreement
Total cost of identity theft to individuals		
Average loss of identity theft to individuals		
Losses of identity theft to businesses, etc.		

2l Find three words or phrases in the extract that the writer uses to show **disagreement** between the sources.

2m Here are some other ways you can show disagreement or differences when synthesizing information from different sources. Underline any words or phrases that indicate differences.

1 With respect to how to solve the problem, Crane (2007) and Friedle (2009) are in complete disagreement.

2 Crane (2007) and Friedle (2009) take different positions with regard to solving the problem.

3 As far as the solution to the problem is concerned, Crane (2007) and Friedle (2009) have opposing views.

4 Different views regarding the solution to the problem are held by Crane (2007) and Friedle (2009).

5 There appear to be differing approaches to solving the problem (e.g. Crane (2007) and Friedle (2009)).

2n Here is part of a report about identity fraud in the USA. Use what you have learned above to complete the text.

> The use of victim information during identity fraud appears to vary widely. Bishop (2007) suggests the most common reason for identity theft is for opening up new credit facilities in the victim's name, with the use of personal information for obtaining new cable and / or utility services also important. Alberg and Johnson (2008) **1)**_____.
>
> **2)**_____ a more recent study by Muldoon (2010) suggests that use of information for use with cheque books and debit card fraud is increasing. Regarding the source of information stolen, **3)**_____ Williamson and Stang (2008) and Browning (2008) found that about one third of cases were started by a person known to the victim. **4)** _____ Nutall (2009) claims that family and friends were the main users of victims' identity details, with identity theft from lost or stolen wallets also important.
>
> Discovery of identity theft appears to vary considerably. Alberg and Johnson (2008) suggest that nearly half of victims found out within the first three months of the crime, **5)**_____ Muldoon (2010) claims that after the same time two thirds had noticed a problem. Nutall (2009) argues that people found out more quickly due to proactive measures taken by banks and businesses, **6)**_____ Alberg and Johnson appeared to find that this was not a major factor.

► LESSON TASK 3 Using synthesis in writing

3a You have been invited to attend a seminar discussion about the impact of violent video games on children. Work in small groups. Discuss these questions.

1 To what extent do you think there is a link between violent video games and violent behaviour in children?

2 Should video games be given 'age-ratings' to restrict their use to people over a certain age?

3b Work in pairs. Each person should read one of the sources on p.112 about the impact of violent video games on children. Read to discover whether these claims are included in your source.

1 That children are in contact with violence in many areas of their lives.

2 That the 'unreal' violence children are in contact with (e.g. on TV or in games) is often more extreme than that they will meet in real life.

3 That children cannot recognize that 'unreal' violence is different from real-world violence.

4 That children can recognize that 'unreal' violence is different from real-world violence.

5 That many video games do not include violence.

6 That violence in video games is becoming increasingly more real.

Source 1

To claim that violent video games lead to real-world violence neglects the fact that the modern child is surrounded by violence. Films, television programmes (for example, both news and sports programmes contain violent images) and even programmes specifically aimed at children such as cartoons contain episodes of violence that are often more violent than anything the child will encounter in their own lives. Clearly most parents recognize that their child understands that these forms of violence are part of another world, beyond their immediate reality. The same holds true for teenagers playing video games. Furthermore, many computer or video games are not violent, with social interaction, logical thinking or role-playing the main focus.

Munning, R. (2002). Video games – fantasy and reality. *Journal of Psychological Research, 13(2)*, 113–124.

Source 2

It was noted earlier that many of today's computer games have violence as a key or central element and that this violence is greater than that met in reality. It should also be noted that this violence is becoming more realistic as games technology develops. In early games, the cartoon images of the main characters, their uneven movements and the poorly designed backgrounds clearly made these games not part of the real world. However, in some of the most recent versions of games, main characters are extremely human, human cries of pain accompany the action and there are graphic and realistic images of blood. All these make it increasingly difficult for children to separate game violence from real-world violence.

Best, D. & Green, K. (2003). *Technology – the hidden dangers*. London: Stairgate Press.

3c Compare your information with your partner.

3d Work in pairs. Use the information from claims 1–6 in 3b to write a short paragraph synthesizing ideas from the two sources. Use the topic sentence below. Make sure any similarities and differences are clearly signposted. Remember that any paraphrasing needs to use your own words, not words or phrases used in the original sources.

Notes
It is not clear exactly to what extent children are influenced by violence in video games. ...

4 Review and extension

4a Underline all the comparing / contrasting language in the following sentences.

1 In contrast to Greig (2005), Mallard (2007) maintains that it is very difficult for parents to completely prevent children from accessing violence online.

2 Greig (2005) argues strongly that parents should play a major role in preventing their children's online access to violence, while Needham and Chetwin (2009) suggest that online filters are usually more effective.

3   Greig (2005) claims it is relatively easy for parents to prevent children visiting unsuitable websites. By contrast, research by Dunbar (2009) suggests that parents are very unsure of their role in this respect.

4   Greig's view therefore contrasts with that of Knowles (2006), who argues that children need to learn to be more independent about making choices about what they access online.

5   Research by Greig (2005) shows that many teenagers are prevented from accessing unsuitable websites by their parents. On the other hand, Mallard (2007) suggests that in fact children often find a way round the restrictions placed on them by their parents.

6   Compared with Greig (2005), Dalton (2007) takes a more critical view of parent involvement in online access.

7   Knowles (2006) argues that children need to learn to be more independent when making choices about what they access online. Similarly, Dalton (2007) highlights the role of the child rather than the parent when selecting online material.

8   According to Greig (2005), teenagers are less likely to access unsuitable online sites after intervention from a parent. A similar idea is put forward by Crowe (2006).

9   Greig (2005) suggests that parents should be more active in preventing online access to violence, whereas Knowles (2006) argues that children need to learn to be more independent about making choices about what they access.

4b Synthesizing and comparing / contrasting sources is done differently, depending on whether it happens over one or two sentences. Look at the sentences in 4a. Put the comparing / contrasting language into groups in this table.

Compare / contrast in one sentence	Compare / contrast over two sentences
At the beginning of the sentence:	
Between the two clauses in the sentence:	

4c Use what you have learned to complete these short texts.

1   Browning (2006) argues that biometric data is more reliable than password data. _____ , a study by Dearing (2008) suggested that, although there were problems with passwords, the use of biometric data was no more reliable.

2   _____ Smithson (2005), Tchsenko (2007) is more positive about the use of fingerprinting at airports.

3   Grosvenor (2005) claims that biometric identity 'cards' would work well, but only if recognition technology is improved. _____ is put forward by Crowe (2006).

4 Bright (2008) discusses the advantages of using biometric systems to society, _____ Newlyn (2004) highlights these from the point of view of the individual.

5 Some research, for example that done by Black (2005), Steadman and Wallace (2006) and Richards (2008), shows that more errors are made with iris recognition technology than with fingerprints. _____, a study by Mills (2007) indicated that fingerprints were more prone to human error.

4d Read these sources. Highlight any ideas which are similar in one colour. Highlight any ideas which are different in another colour.

A

A number of major adult clothing brands are now producing children's or even infant versions of typically 'adult' items, ranging from logo-branded wallets, purses and jewellery to underwear items. From our research, we discovered that over 200 companies which had previously produced adult-only fashions had introduced children's versions of their products between the years 2004 and 2006. What is notable about this is that the items were not, strictly-speaking, children's clothing, but were simply smaller-sized copies (or imitations) of products available in their adult ranges. We suggest that this marks a change in the concept of childhood, which has several implications for the advertising industry.

Robins, G. & Hill, V. (2007). Fashion, identity and market share. *The Journal of Social Economy, 12*(2), 203.

B

Over the past decade, there has been a huge increase in the number of well-known clothing companies marketing products to children. Companies such as Marks & Spencer and Mothercare, traditionally associated with children's clothes, are now in competition with a number of common high street brands formerly seen only as sellers of adult clothing. Many of these have completely rethought the design of children's clothes, bringing in fresh designers to market innovative products that will appeal specifically to this particular market. Instead of simply making smaller versions of clothes worn by adults, these designers have started to bring out clothes that identify children as individuals and fit the needs of children's lives, which can be seen as significantly different from those of most working adults.

Channon, M. (2010). Child-size individuality. *UK Marketing 23*(1), p.48.

4e Write a paragraph synthesizing the sources in 4d.

Notes
There have been significant changes in the fashion industry, especially with regard to children. ...

Reporting in speech

By the end of Part D you will be able to:

- summarize key aspects of research in a presentation
- present an oral argument with alternative viewpoints.

1 Summarizing key aspects of research in a presentation

> When presenting, speakers often give the results of research to support a point in the presentation. However, it may sometimes be important to also give your audience a short summary and more information about the process of that research (what methods were used, which groups of people were researched, and what the purpose of the research was).

1a Work in pairs. Discuss why it might be useful to summarize your research process for your audience.

1b When giving a summary of the research process, it can be helpful to include the following information. Match the type of information (1–5) with its description (a–e).

Part of research process	Description
1 Sample size	a Which specific group of people or items were investigated in the research
2 Sample population	b What research instrument was used (e.g. questionnaire, interview, specific laboratory techniques)
3 Type of sampling used	c How many people or items were investigated in the research
4 Method of data collection	d What the research was intended to discover
5 Research purpose	e How the group of people or items used in the research were chosen (e.g. randomly, or a group with specific characteristics)

3.14

1c Listen to two presenters giving a short summary of the research process for some support they are using. Tick (✓) which information they give.

Part of research process	Speaker 1	Speaker 2
Sample size		
Sample population		
Type of sampling used		
Method of data collection		
Research purpose		

1d Look at these transcripts. In each one, underline:
- the verbs that describe the research process and sample
- the phrase that describes the purpose of the research.

1

On the other hand, a study in 2004 by Waldorf suggests that there is a significant link between real-life violence and video game violence. To find out if video games desensitized children towards real-life violence, 150 US teenagers aged 14–16 were asked a series of interview questions relating to their attitudes towards violence. The results suggested that video game playing was associated with more violent attitudes. However, Waldorf notes that some care needs to be taken with the result because children at this age have little experience of real-life violence.

2

One of the most interesting pieces of evidence showing that facial recognition is indeed reliable comes from a study of eight commercially available facial recognition systems by Bowers and Seymour in 2006. In order to find out how the technology had improved, this research compared each system on its ability to recognize three-dimensional facial images under both controlled and uncontrolled lighting, and compared these to an earlier evaluation done in 2002. The results suggest that face recognition technology appears to have improved dramatically. False recognition rates dropped by 90 per cent and facial recognition technology in the best systems was better than human identification of faces, with accuracy rates near 99 per cent.

1e Work in pairs to finish these sentences.

1 When describing the research process and research sample, speakers often use verbs in _____.

2 When explaining the purpose of a piece of research, speakers often use:
_____.

1f The following table contains verbs and noun phrases often used to describe the research process and research sample. Discuss which verb–noun collocations are acceptable and which ones are not.

analyze	average scores
ask	calculations
calculate	data
carry out	an experiment
choose	an interview
conduct	participants
distribute	a questionnaire
perform	questions
take	samples

1g Write in the verbs that are the most likely collocations for these nouns.

a questionnaire

an interview

an experiment

participants

1h Work in pairs. Each student should choose one of the following two pieces of research. Use what you have learned, and the notes below, to present a brief summary of this research to your partner.

A **Source**: Bright, R. & Thirkettle, S. (2005). Using fingerprints for airport identification. *International Biometrics, 12*(2), 69–83.

Sample size	3,000
Sample population	US domestic air travellers
Type of sampling used	Balance of different nationalities
Method of data collection	Questionnaire
Research purpose	What are passenger attitudes to using fingerprints as a form of passenger identification instead of boarding cards?

B **Source**: Howlett, R. (2007). Parent control of video games in the home. *Parenting UK, 6*, 124–139.

Sample size	200
Sample population	UK parents of 15 year olds
Type of sampling used	Equal number of parents with sons / daughters
Method of data collection	Interview
Research purpose	What limitations (if any) do parents put on their children with regard to use of video games?

2 Presenting an oral argument with alternative viewpoints

3.15

3.16

2a Listen to a speaker give the introduction to a talk on the link between video games and real-world violence. Decide what their position is.

2b Listen to the final part again. Complete the audioscript.

> 1) _____ there has been a lot of research interest in the 2)_____ link between playing games and corresponding violent behaviour in real life, it is 3)_____ that the link between them has 4)_____ been 5)_____ proven yet. 6)_____, there are some suggestive studies which do lead me to believe that such a link 7)_____, and I'd like to offer two reasons to explain that link.

2c Work in pairs. Discuss these questions.

1 Which part of the extract in 2b shows the speaker's position on the topic?

2 Which part of the extract shows an alternative position to the speaker's position?

3 Which comes first – the speaker's own position or the alternative viewpoint? Why?

4 What links the two parts?

5 What words does the speaker use to show their doubt about the alternative position?

6 Why do you think the speaker has included an alternative position as part of the presentation introduction?

7 Which of the following would best replace the first gapped word in 2b?

    Although   At the same time   On the other hand   Over a period of time

2d Work in small groups. Look at the table. Quickly revise some other words or phrases you could use to do these things when presenting an oral argument with alternative viewpoints.

Function	Examples of language
Presenting your own position	I will argue (that) …
Linking your position with an alternative viewpoint	Nevertheless …
Showing doubt about the alternative viewpoint	possible

> Making your own position very clear is often known as 'foregrounding'. In the example in 2b, the speaker has not really emphasized their own position, but if you use alternative viewpoints as part of your argument, or have a strong position, you may wish to do this.

2e Use the phrases below to emphasize your position on these topics.

1 Clothing manufacturers should not market 'adult' fashions to children.

2 The playing of violent video games encourages people to behave violently in real life.

- *In this presentation I / we will argue that …*
- *Throughout this presentation, I / we will suggest that …*
- *In this presentation I / we will try to show (that) …*
- *My own / Our position on this is (that) …*

2f Work in pairs. Choose one of these presentation topics:

1 *The use of biometric identity cards should be encouraged.*

2 *Individual freedom in society belongs only to the rich and powerful.*

2g Work in pairs. Discuss the extent to which you agree with the claim. Give reasons for your position.

2h List one or two alternative viewpoints to your own position.

2i Prepare a short presentation on the topic with your partner.

2j Join another pair of students. Take turns to present your arguments, together with the alternative viewpoints.

3 Including alternative views in a presentation

3a Work in small groups. Brainstorm ideas for a presentation with this title:

A critical evaluation of the use of CCTV.

Notes
<u>Possible advantages of using CCTV for crime prevention in cities</u>
<u>Possible disadvantages of using CCTV for crime prevention in cities</u>

3b Decide on your initial position on the topic. Show your position by marking an 'X' in the appropriate place on these diagrams.

CCTV is a very effective way to reduce crime in cities.   CCTV is a totally ineffective way to reduce crime in cities.

├──┤

CCTV is very cheap.   CCTV is very expensive.

├──┤

Individual privacy is more important than using CCTV for efficient policing.   CCTV helps society, which is more important than individual privacy.

├──┤

3c Discuss the reasons why you hold the positions above.

3d Make a list of any alternative viewpoints to your position.

Notes

3e Design a slide with information to support your position on the topic.

3f Give a presentation of your argument to other members of your class. Include some alternative viewpoints and use the slide to support your own ideas (with source references if necessary).

3g As you listen to other people, focus on how well they explain their argument and integrate the information from the slide into what they say.

4 Review and extension

4a Underline the phrases used to express purpose in a research study in sentences 1–10. An example has been given to help you.

1 A number of different nationalities were used in this study <u>to measure</u> the effectiveness of facial recognition.

2 For the purpose of comparison, two tests were given to the three groups of students.

3 To see if there was a correlation between the two sets of data, the results were plotted on a scattergraph.

4 Participants were interviewed in order that more detail could be obtained on their attitudes.

5 The data was collected online so that it might be more easily analyzed.

6 For the analysis of data, a special statistical package was designed.

7 The teenagers were interviewed separately from their parents so that they would be able to give their own opinions.

8 Short sections of violent video games were shown for the purpose of gaining a direct response.

9 They carried out the same experiment forty times in exactly the same conditions, in order that the results could be considered reliable.

10 A special face recognition scanner was designed for the collection of facial data.

4b Now put the sentences in 4a in pairs, each pair using a similar structure for expressing purpose.

1 _1_ and _3_   **2** _____ and _____   **3** _____ and _____

4 _____ and _____   **5** _____ and _____

4c Work in pairs. Identify the structure of the different pairs and match them with the structures in this table.

Pair	Structure to express purpose in research
1 and 3	*to* + verb (infinitive)
	in order that + (subject) + (modal verb)*
	for the purpose of + noun (or noun phrase)
	for + noun phrase
	so that + (subject) + (modal verb)*

*Although a modal verb is not necessary, it is often used in these structures.

4d Look at these sentences used by presenters speaking about the research process and sample. Complete the sentences with the correct form of the most appropriate verb. You can use each verb more than once.

analyze   ask   calculate   carry out   conduct   distribute   take

1 A survey _____ using international students of mixed nationalities aged between 18 and 22.

2 Questionnaires _____ to participants during class break times.

3 Interviews _____ on a formal basis by one of the research team.

4 The participants _____ a number of questions relating to their attitudes in the form of a questionnaire which _____ online.

5 The data _____ using the common statistical package SPSS 8.0.

6 Hair samples _____ from a number of different patients who had experienced problems.

7 Results for each variable _____ to two decimal places.

3.17

4e Listen to a speaker presenting the information on this slide, which is part of a presentation about the benefits of biometric security systems. What is the speaker's position on the subject?

Security benefits of biometrics system

- ❏ Improves confidence, e.g. electronic payments (Treeth & Ainscough, 2006)

- ❏ Potential to increase privacy by limiting access to personal information (Jewel, Cross & Prabar, 2004)

- ❏ Useful for physical security for high-value customer items, e.g. laptops, mobile phones and cars (Seaman, 2010)

4f Listen again. Make notes in the table on any extra information given about the sources used.

Source	Extra information given by speaker
Treeth & Ainscough, 2006	
Jewel, Cross & Prabar, 2004	
Seaman, 2010	

4g Use this slide and the table on p.124 to prepare a presentation similar to the one in 4e.

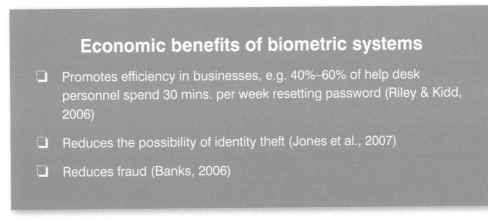

Economic benefits of biometric systems

- ❏ Promotes efficiency in businesses, e.g. 40%–60% of help desk personnel spend 30 mins. per week resetting password (Riley & Kidd, 2006)

- ❏ Reduces the possibility of identity theft (Jones et al., 2007)

- ❏ Reduces fraud (Banks, 2006)

Source	Extra information given by speaker
Riley & Kidd, 2006	Observation study, 30 US businesses (large corporations)
Jones et al., 2007	University of South Wales, online study, 45% less chance of identity fraud with biometric systems compared to passwords
Banks, 2006	Questionnaire, ten EU bank operators

4h Work in pairs. Take turns to deliver your presentation of the slide and information in 4g.

Reporting in writing

By the end of Part E you will be able to:

* identify and use substitution and ellipsis
* identify and use different ways of paraphrasing.

1 Identifying and using substitution and ellipsis

1a Read this passage about biometrics. What words or phrases in the passage do the underlined expressions refer to? Make notes below.

> Each human has a large number of unique physical and behavioural characteristics, including the retina and iris of the eye, hand and fingerprints, the shape of the head or hands, or the spacing between features of the face; even an individual's posture and style of walking are unique. <u>All</u> can be used for biometric identification. <u>This</u> is a growing area of interest in the field of security and personal privacy protection. For businesses and organizations such as banks or online traders, requiring strong security, traditional methods of identification do not guarantee the identity of the individual using them, whereas biometric technology <u>does</u>.

Notes
All:
This:
does:

1b Check your answers with a partner, then discuss why the writer has substituted these phrases rather than repeating them.

> Substitution happens when a writer replaces a previously mentioned word or phrase with a different expression that refers to the same thing.
>
> *Examples*
>
> The **deployment of biometric identification systems by police** is becoming commonplace. Recent examples of **this** ... include the use of biometric iris scanners.
>
> **PIN numbers and signatures** are commonly used for identification, but **neither** is very secure.
>
> This can be done to write more concisely or avoid repetition.

1c Work in pairs. The table below gives examples of words or phrases that are commonly used for substitution. Add the underlined expressions in 1a in the correct space in the table.

Indefinite pronouns	Definite pronouns	Auxiliary verbs
one	she	have
none	it	can
some	those	

1d Work in small groups. Try to think of more words to add to the table.

1e Read the extract below, paying attention to the underlined expressions (1–5). Then decide which of the words in the box can be used to substitute each underlined word or phrase.

half   do   few   this   ones

The use of biometric technologies is clearly on the increase, but there is still some question about public acceptance. Ultimately, **1)** public acceptance, not cost, could determine whether biometric ID methods are widely adopted. Differences in the areas of the body scanned by biometric systems could cause users to reject **2)** systems which they feel invade their privacy. In a recent study of public attitudes to biometrics, while approximately 70 per cent of the respondents claimed that they felt comfortable using biometric scans of the hand, only **3)** 50 per cent of the respondents claimed that they were comfortable with scans of the eye, and **4)** only about 10 per cent of the respondents would be willing to submit to a full body scan. Concerns were raised not only about privacy, but also about security: most respondents in the survey said they expected a biometric system to operate without any mistakes, though in fact at the moment, no functioning biometric systems **5)** operate without mistakes.

1f Add any new substitution words to the table in 1c.

> *Ellipsis* happens when a writer leaves out a word or phrase which can be understood from the context. The benefits of using ellipsis in this way are the same as those for substitution: the writer can paraphrase the work of others, express ideas more concisely and avoid monotonous repetition.
>
> **1** Elision of phrases after an indefinite pronoun.
>
> *Example*
>
> ***None*** ~~*of them*~~ *are currently in use.*
>
> **2** Elision of a previously mentioned or understood word or phrase.
>
> *Example*
>
> *Acuity supports this claim, noting that the* **biometrics market** *has enjoyed strong growth in the first years of the 21st century and predicting sustained growth of the* **~~biometrics~~ market** *at least to the year 2020.*

1g Read the passage below and use ellipsis to shorten the underlined expressions.

> Biometric identification is commonly perceived as being a potential future technology. In fact, most <u>biometric identification systems</u> are already technically possible, and <u>many of them</u> are already in use in one form or another around the world. For instance, effective fingerprint scanning systems have been technically and economically feasible for a number of years now, and these systems are increasingly used for room security in large corporations. Indeed, <u>several systems</u> are already in use on ATM machines in Japan. However, there remain obstacles to widespread adoption of biometric ID systems. <u>All of them</u> are expensive when compared with more conventional identification systems, such as ID cards, signatures and PIN numbers, and <u>each one</u> has its own technical limitations, ranging from the size of the scanner needed, to the accuracy of its scans. A further issue is public acceptance: while acceptance studies have provided a great deal of information about how people would respond to different types of biometric system, <u>less information</u> is known about the accuracy levels that the public would demand in order to feel that the systems were safe.

1h Check your answers with a partner.

1i The two paragraphs below are from academic texts. Underline or show where either ellipsis or substitution has taken place.

Paragraph 1

> Banks, petrol stations, chain stores, transportation centres, public and private office buildings, shopping malls, universities, schools, hospitals, museums, sports arenas, residential areas have one thing in common: all have CCTV surveillance systems. However, the extent of CCTV differs from country to country. Our findings suggest that its diffusion in semi-public space is most advanced in Britain, where we found 40% of the studied publicly accessible locations under surveillance.

Paragraph 2

> In Sheffield, for example, the Sheffield Wide Image Switching System, or SWISS, which was launched in 2003, has a control room staffed 24 hours a day and can now control around 150 publicly funded cameras covering the city centre streets. However, SWISS has also integrated other public and privately owned camera systems, including those of an out-of-town shopping mall, tram system and university. In doing so, the system is much more efficient than each organization running its own system.

1j Below are two paragraphs from academic texts which have been adapted to demonstrate what a text might look like without the use of ellipsis or substitution. Rewrite the two paragraphs (A and B) more efficiently, using ellipsis, substitution and making any other necessary changes.

A

However, biometrics have also proved themselves useful in providing physical security for high value consumer items such as laptops, mobile phones and cars. High value consumer items such as laptops, mobile phones and cars can be securely locked by biometric fingerprint scans and by securely locking the biometrics present no opportunity to even the most enterprising of thieves. Locking biometrics has helped to raise public confidence about consumer biometrics and, alongside the perhaps 'sexy' image that this technology enjoys (Biometric Technology Today, 2006, p.8), has contributed to a great deal of enthusiastic acceptance of its introduction.

Rewrite

B

Government agencies can also claim credit for helping to popularize biometric technologies. Identity theft is a serious threat for official government services, everything from tax returns to applications for driving licences and passports. Tax returns, applications for driving licences, passports and so on, as a result, require strong ID authentication measures to guard against the serious risk of criminal misuse of such sensitive data. A large (and steadily increasing) number of government departments have started inviting citizens to enrol biometric data such as fingerprints or DNA. In inviting citizens to enrol biometric data such as fingerprints or DNA, official work is made more efficient (identification becomes faster) but also more secure against the risk of fraud.

Rewrite

1k Compare your answers with a partner.

2 Identifying and using different ways of paraphrasing

2a Text A below is from a source article on social trends and the growth of CCTV. Text B is a paraphrased version of it used in an essay. Read the two texts. Highlight any information in Text B that is also in Text A.

A

Social trends and the growth of CCTV

CCTV technology is being used in an ever-widening number of public spaces. Despite claims by civil rights campaigners that this represents a serious and deliberate attack on privacy rights by authoritarian governments, it seems in fact to be a natural response by law enforcement agencies to the problem of anonymity in massive, globalized, urban communities.

(Clarkson, P. (2009). Understanding the rise in CCTV in the UK. *Surveillance Issues Bulletin*, 6(3),p.37.)

B

CCTV is increasingly becoming a common feature of public life. However, many people are suspicious of the idea that the police or security guards can monitor the general public 24 hours a day. However, Clarkson (2009, p.37) suggests that even though civil rights campaigners argue that CCTV is a major and intentional assault on the right to privacy by governments which want to control their populations, the use of CCTV technology is simply a logical thing for the police to do because of the fact that globalization and urbanization make it more difficult for them to recognize people.

2b Now look at the similarities and differences in more detail. How have the words and phrases from Text A been paraphrased in Text B? Complete the middle column of the table below.

	Text A	Text B	Type of paraphrase
1	CCTV technology	CCTV	
2	is being used		
3	widening number		
4	public spaces		
5	Despite		
6	claims		
7	serious and deliberate		
8	attack		
9	authoritarian governments		
10	a natural response		
11	law enforcement agencies		
12	the problem of anonymity		
13	globalized, urbanized		

> When paraphrasing, one method is to define specific or technical vocabulary from the source text.
>
> ***Example***
> Source: *information about how people would respond to **different types of biometric system**.*
>
> Paraphrase: *data regarding public reaction to **security systems which use fingerprints, eye scanning or voice recognition**.*

2c Now match the method with the words and clauses from texts A and B in 2a. Write the methods in the right-hand column of the table in 2b. You may not need all of the methods.

different linking words   ellipsis   noun phrases   passive / active
synonyms   word class   word definitions

> **LESSON TASK**   **3 Paraphrasing a text**

3a Read this paragraph about CCTV. Identify the authors' claims.

Due to a rising population, cities are growing, and people are travelling around their own countries as well as abroad. Police forces have difficulty tracing criminals and terrorists among the faceless inhabitants in today's metropolises. As other organizations, law enforcement agencies have to work efficiently with the assets they have, and CCTV aids the police in this effectiveness.

(Humbert, D., & Manson, P. (2005). *Safety and Security in Cities*. Cambridge: Delves Publications.)

3b Check your answers with a partner.

3c Paraphrase the text to support the point below using different techniques.

Notes
The use of CCTV may be beneficial, especially in urban environments....

3d Work in pairs. Swap your paraphrased texts. Compare key words and / or phrases to the original source. Identify the changes made in terms of ellipsis, synonyms, word order, etc. Use the table on p.131.

	Source text	Paraphrased text	Type of paraphrase
1			
2			
3			
4			
5			
6			
7			
8			
9			
10			
11			
12			

3e Work in small groups. Tell each other what you have found out about your analysis of your partner's text. Decide which paraphrased text is the most effective and why.

4 Review and extension

4a Read this text. What is the writer's main idea?

> Closed-Circuit Television (CCTV) is becoming ever more common in the world's cities. However, the extent to which CCTV is deployed differs from country to country. In a report prepared for the European Commission, the Urbaneye project indicated that around 300 CCTV systems were monitoring public space in France, compared to just 30 systems in Germany and **none** in Denmark (Urbaneye, 2004, p.61). However, the Urbaneye study observed that by far the largest number of CCTV systems were to be found in the UK, with about 40,000 cameras 'in more than 500 cities' (ibid).
>
> Not only is CCTV monitoring more common in the UK, but **it** tends to be more technically sophisticated. Many organizations use separate CCTV systems, but the tendency in the UK is to integrate **these** under the control of a single organization, which can monitor **them all** simultaneously.

4b Identify the words or phrases that each word in **bold** refers to.

> Expressions beginning with 'do' can be substituted for longer verb phrases to make writing more concise. For example:
>
> | 'Do' expression | Meaning |
> |---|---|
> | Do so | Perform an action already mentioned in the text |
> | Do similarly / do likewise | Perform the same action as that performed by someone else |

4c Choose the best 'Do' expression to complete this text (you may need to change the form of the verb).

> The increasing anonymity and swelling populations of large modern cities make efficient policing ever more difficult. It is unsurprising, then, that many nations are increasingly looking towards adopting CCTV and biometric technologies to support policing. Some nations such as the UK and France have already **1)** _____ extensively, while other nations such as Germany have introduced more limited systems. Given obvious cost and efficiency benefits, it is likely that many other nations will **2)** _____ in future. However, while CCTV technology is popular and widely used in some nations, in other nations it is not popular or widely used. Despite the possible attractions of CCTV and biometric technologies from the point of view of the authorities, some nations may find themselves unable to install widespread public CCTV systems due to cultural attitudes to privacy. Any attempt to **3)** _____ might meet with stiff public resistance.

> Ellipsis is particularly common in comparisons. Expressions following auxiliary verbs or 'be' expressions can be elided to make writing more concise.
>
> ***Examples***
>
> *PIN numbers **cannot guarantee the identity of the person using them**; iris scans, however, **can** ~~guarantee the identity of the person using them~~.*
>
> *A signature **is not secure**, but biometric scanning **is** ~~secure~~.*

4d Read the text in 4c again and identify any expressions which can be elided.

4e The extract below is 245 words long. Rewrite the text in the space opposite, using substitution and ellipsis to reduce the word count and avoid repetition.

With an eye to the future of biometric identification, we can predict that technological improvements will continue to propel growth in the area of biometric identification, despite claims from some critics that biometric identification systems are not reliable enough. The reliability of biometric scanning is in fact already very high, though it remains true that any current biometric scanning system will incorrectly recognize a proportion of unauthorized users (or reject legitimate users). Incorrect recognition of unauthorized users and rejection of legitimate users is due to environmental and physical factors. For instance, with face recognition technology, light or darkness can impact the quality of the reading, as can the angle at which the individual stands in response to the reader. Scans of the iris or retina currently require the subject individual to position themselves precisely in relation to the scanner and can also be confounded by people wearing dark glasses or contact lenses. Even fingerprint scans are not currently foolproof. However, as biometric scanning technology improves we can expect to see biometric systems having consistently better recognition rates, which will encourage consumer and business confidence in using the technology to secure financial transactions (and companies which use the technology to secure financial transactions will enjoy a better reputation for security with customers). It is likely that, as we move towards a cashless economy in which all goods and services are bought and paid for electronically, biometric systems will come to replace PINS, passwords and signatures entirely.

Rewrite

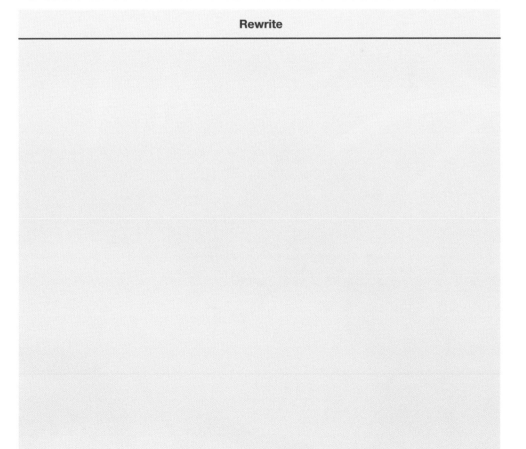

Unit 4 Choices

Unit overview

Part	This part will help you to …	By improving your ability to …
A	**Listen critically**	• identify and understand repetition • identify and understand reformulation • identify stance markers.
B	**Critically evaluate logic in texts**	• identify emphasis in academic texts • identify and understand analogy in academic texts.
C	**Develop as an independent learner**	• identify common errors in formality levels of academic emails • understand appropriate features of emails in different situations • identify formal and informal language in written communication.
D	**Conclude a presentation**	• conclude an oral presentation • speculate about research results in conclusions.
E	**Conclude, review and edit an essay**	• develop language for writing conclusions • refer to previous sections of an academic text in the conclusion • express importance, desirability and necessity.

Understanding spoken information

By the end of Part A you will be able to:

- identify and understand repetition
- identify and understand reformulation
- identify stance markers.

1 Identifying and understanding repetition

1a Work in pairs. Discuss these questions.

1   What are some of the advantages of having choice as a consumer?

2   What are some of the disadvantages?

1b Work in pairs. Read this introduction to an academic lecture on choice. Guess what phrases might complete the gaps.

> I'd like to tell you today about some of the things that can affect the way you make choices in your life. Now, if you're like me, then you probably enjoy living in a society where you have plenty of options available to you. **1)** _____ varieties of coffee in your local coffee shop, and if you don't like plain coffee, then you have **2)** _____ alternative toppings to try. Supermarket shelves stacked with, say, **3)** _____ versions of each product, to suit any taste or budget. If you want to buy an item of clothing, then you can choose between **4)** _____ of stores to find the thing you like best.

1c Listen and complete the extract from the lecture in 1b.

4.1

> Speakers can try to help their listeners to understand more easily by using repetition: the speaker attempts to make the links between different ideas clearer by expressing them again in similar ways, or repeats key ideas in order to emphasize their importance. This can be done by repeating similar words, phrases or even grammatical structures.

1d Look again at the text in 1b. Work in pairs. Discuss what phrases 1–4 have in common.

1e Suggest some advantages and potential problems for listeners if a speaker repeats or reformulates information in a lecture or presentation. Make notes in the space below.

Notes

1f Look at the next extract from the same academic lecture. Work in pairs. Complete the text with these phrases (a–e).

   a that one thing which your boss asks you to do

   b Great, more choice

   c it gives us a satisfying feeling that we are in control of what we are doing

   d we've all

   e So there's something in us, basically, that likes to be given a choice

Nicola Bown and colleagues studied the way shoppers make decisions and found that people tend to choose an option more often when it is offered alongside an alternative than when it's simply presented by itself. **1)**_____. I know this is going to seem like a daft question, but what is it exactly that we like about having choices? A number of behavioural psychologists claim that this is related to the feeling of control it gives us. We like choice because **2)** _____. To illustrate this with one example from the world of work, imagine your boss gives you a task to perform, and you have no choice about it, just **3)** _____. Well, psychological studies show that most people are going to resent it. If the boss gives two jobs and tells you to choose which one to do first – gives you some freedom, in other words – then you're likely, according to the research, to be more motivated, and more satisfied. So we associate choice with freedom, with control over our own lives.

But there's a problem. Some choice is good, yes. Let's imagine that you're buying a pair of socks, and you go to the shop and there are, say, five pairs to choose from. **4)** _____. But what happens when you raise the number of choices available from five to ten, or fifteen, or more than twenty? That's exactly what one study by Sheena Iyengar and Mark Lepper set out to discover. They set up booths in a grocery store, one offering six different kinds of jam, and the other offering twenty-four kinds. And what did they find? That more people chose to buy jam from the booth offering only six choices. A number of other similar studies have found comparable results: that there is a threshold above which it becomes very difficult for a person to make a decision, and in which case they are unlikely to make any choice *at all*. I expect you all understand this, **5)** _____ experienced it, and maybe for most of us it's a minor irritation – the time it takes to choose which pair of shoes you want, all those buttons you choose not to use on your TV remote control.

4.2

1g Now listen to the extract and check your answers.

1h Work in pairs. Discuss which information the repetitions in 1f (a–e) refer back to. Then discuss the function of each. Complete this table.

Function of repetition / reformulation	Example (a–e)
To emphasize a particular situation	
To make reasons / explanations clearer	
To summarize previous information	

1i Read this extract from a lecture in which a speaker identifies factors that can affect the way people make choices. Guess what words and phrases might complete the gaps.

Now in any situation where somebody is faced with a choice, presumably they have a goal of some sort, and that goal can vary a lot depending on the circumstances. So let's say, you want to buy a new car. One person's goal may be to buy the most economical car available, the cheapest one out there. Another person, though, might have a different goal, say – to buy **1)**_____ luxurious car, or **2)**_____ environmentally friendly, or the fastest one, whatever. So the goal sets the framework for the decision. When you make your choice, you're trying to do so in a way that gets you closest to your **3)**_____, in the most satisfying way.

The situation, of course, can affect the goal. Let's say that you're looking for a car, and are hoping for a luxurious one, but price is a problem because you don't have much money. So there **4)**_____ – not having money – affects the goal, changing it from getting a luxurious car to getting the most luxurious car that I can afford. So **5)**_____ .

Now, what factors are going to affect the decision in a positive way, which get us as close to the goal as possible? Firstly, I suppose, a successful outcome – a **6)**_____ choice, that is – depends on how well the individual is able to calculate all the benefits and drawbacks to the decision. Most choices, really, are of this sort – it's very rare that you have to make a straightforward decision between, say, just two things without having to consider anything else. There are normally multiple issues **7)**_____ , and those people who are able to consider all of the variables rationally are often believed to be better at making reliable decisions.

Experience can also affect the success of a decision. If you're buying a house for the second or third time, for instance, you will have more **8)**_____ and knowledge of the important things **9)**_____ than someone who's buying a house for the first time. So **10)**_____ .

1j Check your answers with a partner.

4.3

1k Listen to the original extract and find out how the speaker employed repetition. How was it different from your ideas?

2   Identifying and understanding reformulation

A speaker giving an unscripted speech will sometimes feel that they have not expressed an idea in the most satisfactory way, so it is common for speakers to reformulate phrases: they restate ideas using different expressions.

2a Work in pairs. The third sentence below is a reformulation of the idea explained in the first two sentences. Think of expressions that you could use to signpost the reformulation.

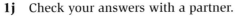

The psychologists Sheena Iyengar and Mark Lepper have identified a phenomenon they describe as 'choice overload'. Basically, choice overload is the situation where it becomes nearly impossible to distinguish between options when the person choosing is presented with too many. _____, it becomes more difficult to make decisions as the number of choices increases.

2b Listen to the speaker and make a note of the expression the speaker uses.

4.4

2c Work in small groups. Brainstorm expressions that a speaker can use to signpost reformulation. Make a note of them in the space below.

Expressions for reformulation

2d Listen and complete the extracts from a lecture with the reformulation expressions which the speaker uses.

4.5

A study of the way in which shoppers make decisions discovered that consumers tend to choose options most often when they are offered alongside an alternative choice. So, **1)**_____, people enjoy having a range of options.

Some researchers claim that individuals prefer choice because it gives them a sense of control; it makes us feel that we are in charge of our lives, **2)** _____.

Imagine your boss gives you a task to perform, and you have no choice about it, just that one thing which your boss asks you to do. Well, psychological studies show that most people are going to resent it. If the boss gives two jobs and tells you to choose which one to do first – gives you some freedom, **3)** _____ – then you're likely, according to the research, to be more motivated.

The so-called 'tyranny of choice' is pretty easy to understand; we've all experienced it. It becomes increasingly difficult to make choices as the number of options increases. **4)** _____, we tend to find confusing decisions stressful.

So here's a basic framework for understanding the way we make decisions. You can think of this in terms of four things: the goal, the situation, the factors contributing to the best decision, and finally the factors which interfere with the decision – which can cause the decision to be less accurate, **5)** _____.

A successful decision outcome – a successful choice, **6)** _____ – is the result of a calculation of a number of different factors.

4.6

2e Listen to an extract from a lecture about choice overload. How does the speaker use reformulation to explain each of these things? Make notes below.

1 Maximizer

2 Satisficer

Notes

3 Identifying stance markers

> A speaker's stance is their attitude or point of view on the information that they are giving. Speakers often help their audience to understand their stance by using clear expressions to foreground it. Stance expressions can be used to:
>
> **1** express an emotional response
> **2** make strong claims seem less assertive
> **3** make a claim seem stronger.
>
> ***Examples***
> **1** *People often think that more choice is always good but, **surprisingly**, research shows the opposite is the case.*
> **2** *There is, **to be honest**, little evidence for this.*
> **3** *Individuals **clearly** find it difficult to make a decision when faced with too many choices.*

3a Work in small groups. Put these stance markers into the correct spaces in the table.

basically   I must say   in fact   naturally   obviously   regrettably
to be honest   understandably   unsurprisingly

Expressing an emotional response	Making claims less assertive	Making claims stronger

4.7

3b Listen and complete this excerpt from later in the lecture on decision-making styles with the stance markers that the speaker uses. Then check your answers with a partner.

So, 1)_____ we can all be put somewhere on a line between extreme maximizers and extreme satisficers. Think about it – which type of decision maker are you? Now the next point of my talk today is that the decision-making style that you tend to adopt can have important impacts on your behaviour and psychological condition. Now, 2)_____, if you struggle to make decisions, then it's going to decrease your happiness, and, 3)_____, we find that maximizers, overall, report much lower ratings of happiness with life than satisficers do. That's 4)_____, I think. But recent research reveals some other interesting things too. Firstly, maximizers tend to experience strong feelings of regret more often than satisficers, probably because they spend time after making a decision worrying about whether they made the best choice, and often thinking they've missed out. What is very 5)_____, however, is that recent research indicates that maximizers *don't* actually behave the way we expect them to when they make decisions. The expectation is that maximizers always spend a long time considering choices carefully before reaching a decision, but, in fact, a 2007 study by Andrew Parker and colleagues in Pittsburgh suggested that maximizers *don't* always spend very long making decisions in the first place – 6)_____, the evidence suggests that they tend to worry intensely, make a snap decision which they haven't thought through very carefully, and *then* worry about whether they made the right decision afterwards. 7)_____, I'm a bit like that myself.

3c Work in pairs. Express your own stance on each of these issues to your partner, using stance markers to indicate your opinion. Give reasons to support your stance.

1 The reasons why e-commerce (shopping online) is increasingly popular
2 The ease of shopping online

3d Now listen to a speaker talk about the same points. Make a note of the speaker's stance on each point. Then check your answers with a partner.

4.8

Notes

4   Identifying a speaker's stance on a topic

4a   Work in small groups. Discuss these questions.

   1   What are the factors worth considering when choosing a course in higher education?

   2   Which do you think would be the most important factors?

   3   What other sources of information might be considered when making a decision?

4b   You are going to listen to an extract from a short lecture on choosing an institute of higher education after leaving school. Decide your position on these issues. Show it by marking an 'X' in the appropriate place.

Choosing a higher education course is quite simple.	Choosing a higher education course is very difficult.

The huge choice of institutes of higher education and courses is advantageous to would-be students.	The huge choice of institutes of higher education and courses is disadvantageous to would-be students.

All school leavers should consider going on to higher education.	Higher education is often a waste of time for many school leavers.

4.9

4c   Compare your position with other students, giving reasons for your answers.

4d   Listen to the extract from the lecture. Identify the speaker's stance on the issues above. Mark them on the lines with a small circle.

4e   Check your answers with a partner. Explain what helped you to decide on the speaker's stance.

4f   During the extract, the speaker repeated and reformulated pieces of information. Work in pairs. Complete the text on p.142 by reformulating the underlined words or phrases.

A higher education was once the preserve of the rich. However, a half century of increasing affluence overall, and a general spread of that **1)**_____ throughout all levels of society, has resulted in greater numbers of students than ever before aspiring to a higher education. I would like to investigate some of the consequences of this from the viewpoint of psychologist Barry Schwartz's 'tyranny of choice' theory.

What Schwartz terms the tyranny of choice is the familiar struggle that most of us experience with an ever greater number of consumer choices available to us. It becomes ever more difficult to **2)**_____, and ever more difficult to remain satisfied with _____ that we do make when we regretfully compare them afterwards with the _____ we might've made instead.

As Schwartz himself has observed, this phenomenon is increasingly apparent in the decision that school leavers face about whether to **3)** _____ or carry on with education. It is something of a vicious circle, in fact. As the pool of potential students grows, so competition between universities for the best students increases, leading these universities, in turn, to try to appeal to future students by increasing the range of courses, accommodation and extra-curricular activities available. More **4)** _____, more _____. This explosion of options can make it very difficult for the student to make a reasonable choice about the most important thing – to stay **5)** _____ or _____ after school.

The would-be student must consider a range of factors when deciding whether to go on to higher education or not. Students must compare the relative merits of **6)** _____ with going _____. If you leave school, you can begin working earlier, and work your way up the career ladder earlier, whereas if you **7)** _____, maybe you hope that earning a degree will help you to secure more satisfying work or a better salary at the end of it. School leavers, and often their parents, must make **8)** _____ about the financial, career and personal costs of either option, weighing them against what they might miss if they make the 'wrong' decision.

4g Listen to the lecture extract again. Compare your reformulations and repetitions with the speaker's.

4h Prepare a two-minute talk on one of these subjects. Remember to repeat and reformulate important points.

Choosing:

1 a job

2 to study at home or go abroad to study

3 consumer goods.

4i Give your talk to others as part of a small group. Ask them to make notes on the main points. Check their notes and make sure they have written all of the key points.

5 Review and extension

5a Below is the audioscript from the introduction to a short academic lecture about decision-making. Complete the extract with the phrases in the box. The phrases are examples of repetition or reformulation. Use the underlined sections of the text to help you.

> in each decision   you make decisions   make our choices
> complexity of life in the 21st century   a process of some sort

We live in <u>a very complex world</u>, and each of us faces a number of situations in which we have to make decisions every day. In fact, it's probably no exaggeration to say that the sheer number of choices we face every day is increasing, with the growing **1)** _____. The question is, how do <u>we go about making these decisions</u>? Do **2)** _____, even the most complex and serious ones, on gut feeling, or do you have <u>a system</u>, **3)** _____, that allows you to think through all the factors involved **4)** _____ and be sure that you have <u>made the best choice</u>? Are there rules that govern the way we **5)** _____? And if so, what are they?

5b Listen to the excerpt from the lecture and check your answers.

4.10

5c Listen to a speaker explain their ideas about the tyranny of choice. Make a note of the stance words that the speaker uses for each of these points.

1 Having more choice is a good thing.

2 Some people are more affected by the tyranny of choice.

3 The extent to which the tyranny of choice problem affects everyone.

4.11

5d Decide which of these statements describes the speaker's likely opinion on the topic.

1 There is no evidence to support the theory of the tyranny of choice.

2 The tyranny of choice problem only affects some people.

3 The tyranny of choice problem affects everyone.

Stance markers such as *to be honest* and *frankly* make bold claims appear less assertive. However, these claims are still strong. Many English speakers prefer to avoid making direct, bold claims, so they soften them with preparatory phrases such as these. Nevertheless, these phrases do not weaken the strength of the claim or leave room for doubt about what the speaker believes. In effect, phrases such as these also emphasize the speaker's opinion.

4.12

5e Listen to the next extract from the lecture about the tyranny of choice. What strong opinions does the speaker have?

5f Use a dictionary to find out what these stance words mean. Make a note of them in your vocabulary logbook.

    a incredibly

    b astonishingly

    c critically

    d incomprehensibly

    e fundamentally

    f bafflingly

    g plausibly

Understanding written information

By the end of Part B you will be able to:

- identify emphasis in academic texts
- identify and understand analogy in academic texts.

1 Identifying emphasis in academic texts

Academic English tends to be written in an impersonal and cautious way, as writers use evidence to make claims for which they may not be certain. However, sometimes a writer will wish to emphasize a point, or express stronger confidence in a claim. Emphasis can be achieved by:

a using emphatic words and expressions
b rearranging the structure of information in a sentence.

1a Read the following text from an academic journal, in response to a previous article. Work in pairs. Discuss these questions.

1 What appears to be Barlow's position on climate change?

2 What appears to be Hollis's position on climate change?

3 Why does Barlow feels that Hollis has attacked his position unfairly?

Hollis (2009, p.848) attacks my argument for confirming climate change trends on the grounds that I have adopted 'extreme' evidence and 'unlikely' climate change models to support my views. However, Hollis himself frequently uses only the most extremely optimistic risk models to support his own views.

Barlow, N. (2010). Comments: In answer to Graeme Hollis. *Climate Letters*, *15*(1), 1119.

1b Underline the word that Barlow uses in the text above to emphasize to the reader that Hollis has used information that he has previously criticized.

Reflexive pronouns (e.g. *himself / herself, myself, themselves*) can be used to emphasize a particular person or subject doing an action. For example, the second sentence below puts more emphasis on both the action and the fact that it is Hollis performing the action:

1 Hollis frequently uses only the most extremely optimistic risk models to support his own views.
2 Hollis **himself** frequently uses only the most extremely optimistic risk models to support his own views.

1c Complete these with a reflexive pronoun to add emphasis.

1 Those nations which criticize our policy of oil exploration on the grounds that it heightens the risk of climate change would do well to remember that we are only doing what is in the interest of our economic development. Many of those nations which criticize us have _____ achieved their wealth through the same means and it is hypocritical to place responsibility for climate change risks on us now.

2

Taylor (1999) attacks my suggestion that people engaging in risky sports should pay higher premiums for their insurance. According to Taylor, this would be an unfair burden on a legitimate lifestyle choice (1999, p.203). However, Taylor _____ has made claims of a similar sort in the past (see, for instance, Taylor 1991a; 1991b; 1994).

3

As Schwartz and Hopkins _____ have observed, this phenomenon is increasingly apparent in the decision that school leavers face about whether to leave school or carry on with education into university.

1d Discuss which specific actions are being emphasized in the texts above.

1e Complete these sentences with an appropriate reflexive pronoun to emphasize the things *in italics* or the actions they are performing.

    1 Since the criticism from outside of some of the methods used, *the research team* _____ has realized that things could have been more controlled.

    2 *The idea* _____ is interesting; it's unfortunate that the book fails to support it fully.

    3 *The respondents* _____ complained that the research process did not seem to be logical.

    4 Although the experiment was undertaken some time ago, even *we* _____ didn't know the full results until last week.

1f Work in small groups. Discuss other ways a speaker or writer can emphasize what they are saying. Make notes of your ideas.

Notes

1g Read these extracts from academic textbooks. Underline the words and phrases in each which help to emphasize certain information.

A

Some of these claims may rightly be dismissed as speculation, but what is undeniable is that biometrics is here to stay, and that its use is only likely to become more widespread. It will increasingly impact our lives in the years to come.

B Climate change presents an almost unimaginable challenge to the prosperity, comfort, health and even survival of our societies. It is now perfectly clear that this is a threat unlike any our species has ever faced before, bringing the risk of nations disappearing under the seas, mass dislocation of refugees, food shortages and the destruction of our precious ecosystem. The evidence shows conclusively that if we do not wish to see a world changed beyond all recognition and one in which humankind will undergo huge suffering, then we must all act now. The choices we make today, such as immediately replacing dirty carbon fuels (for example, oil and coal) with nuclear energy and the development of non-carbon transport systems, are essential if we are not to suffer a similar fate to that of the dinosaurs who became extinct millions of years ago.

Even though academic writing tends to avoid making strong claims, writers will sometimes try to emphasize claims on which they are particularly confident, using so-called 'boosting expressions'.

Example

*The evidence shows **clearly** that the Earth is not warming.*

Boosting expressions are used to give the impression that a claim is based on facts or is so plainly true that it cannot be denied.

1h Read these text extracts and identify the boosting expressions that the writer uses.

A Recent behavioural studies have demonstrated plainly that individuals tend to underestimate risk. This is certainly apparent in situations where the risks are remote in time or space.

B Without doubt, industrial design which pays attention to decision-making ease by operators can help to reduce time spent on decisions. There is obviously a need, therefore, for better design of aircraft and machinery control systems to reduce the danger of accidents caused by so-called 'choice overload'.

C Accurate decision-making abilities are indisputably critical for emergency service personnel. As a consequence, we advise that front line fire, police and ambulance teams receive decision-making training. We argue that such training will inevitably result in better performance by emergency workers.

D The number of options which a consumer faces affects their ability to feel satisfied with their purchasing decisions (see, for instance, Iyengar and Lepper, 2000.) However, questions definitely remain about whether an 'optimum' number of choices exists.

E It is often assumed that individuals making decisions do so by rationally evaluating all of the factors involved in the decision. In some situations this is no doubt the case, though it is unlikely to be true with all decision situations. What is certain, however, is that most individuals tend to rely on 'gut-feeling' to help them make decisions.

F The evidence presented above suggests that we are faced with serious questions about the best way to manage our natural resources in the coming half century. Increasing population will put more stress on existing water, food, energy and industrial supplies. While these problems are undoubtedly significant, they can nevertheless be overcome through planning, preparation and coordination of government with industry and local communities.

1i Check your answers with a partner.

1j Read the two texts below and answer these questions:

    1 What claims do the writers make?

    2 How confident are the writers about these claims?

A Many models of how individuals make choices assume a rational basis for their decision. However, psychological evidence indicates that individuals tend not to make their decisions in this way.

B Research evidence clearly shows that individuals tend not to make decisions using solely rational techniques. Instead, most people tend to 'go by their instincts' when making choices. However, what is indisputable is that training in using strict rational decision-making methods can help to improve the quality of those choices.

> Information can also be emphasized by changing the word order of sentences. It is common in English to place more important information towards the end of a sentence.

1k Work in pairs. Discuss which information is most emphasized.

    1 The most in-depth research into manager decision-making processes was carried out by Professor Dillon's team in 2008, using managers from 87 different UK companies.

    2 Using managers from 87 different UK companies, the most in-depth research into manager decision-making processes was carried out by Professor Dillon's team in 2008.

    3 In 2008, using managers from 87 different UK companies, Professor Dillon's team carried out the most in-depth research into manager decision-making processes.

> Though the most common way to order information in English is to move from less important information at the beginning of a sentence to more important at the end, writers can sometimes achieve emphasis by deliberately reversing this order using an *it* + *be* structure with a relative pronoun.
>
> ***It was*** Professor Dillon's team ***that*** *carried out the most in-depth research into manager decision-making processes, using managers from 87 different UK companies.*
>
> The information placed between *it* and the relative pronoun (in this case, *that*) is the information which is emphasized.

1l Rewrite these sentences using *it* and emphasizing the underlined information.

   1 Most people make choices by <u>trusting their instincts</u>.

   2 The thing that makes decision-making difficult is <u>having too many choices</u>.

   3 The person who first claimed that climate change was a myth was <u>Carl Marston</u>.

2 Identifying and understanding analogy in academic texts

> An **analogy** is a comparison between things which have similar features, and which is often used to help explain a principle or idea.

2a Identify the analogies in these texts.

A
In emergency situations people must often make life-or-death decisions very rapidly. Risk analysis is the process by which a person calculates possible risks, then compares them with so-called mitigating factors – those factors in a situation which can reduce the danger involved. In normal situations this is simple enough: the human mind is well-adapted to making such calculations. However, as the situation becomes more complex, or more dangerous, and a quick decision becomes necessary, the human mind, like the CPU on a computer, can be overloaded by tasks and fail to reach a timely decision about what to do.

B
Making decisions in a crisis is something like driving a car. The driver must handle a large amount of information about the world around them while simultaneously operating a number of controls to guide the car to where they want to go.

2b Look more carefully at the grammar of the analogies below. In pairs, discuss any similarities and differences.

   1 *the human mind* + *[is]* + *like* + *the CPU on a computer* + explanation / extension

   2 *making decisions* + *is* + *like* + *driving a car* + explanation / extension

2c *Like* is not the only word used to show analogy in academic writing. Identify the analogies in these texts and circle the phrases the writer has used to signpost the analogy.

A

Management decisions are often made in the same way that a tennis player plays a tennis shot. Every decision is the last part of a series of actions, although many decision makers, similar to tennis players, are unaware of the steps that precede the final decision.

B

One way of viewing decision-making is as a computer game with no end. However many characters you kill with each decision, there are always more waiting to be disposed of in a never-ending stream.

C

Making the choice about which university to go to can be compared to walking in a dark room. Most school leavers stumble around not knowing or seeing very much, bump into something that does not hurt too much and are then horrified to find out what they have chosen when the lights go on.

D

Managers can be seen as football coaches. They help players understand what decisions need to be made and when, and, by doing this, help to realize an individual's full potential to play an integral part in the company team.

2d Work in pairs. Think of and write analogies for each of these topics.
  1 doing homework
  2 writing an academic essay
  3 learning English

2e In pairs, compare your analogies.

> A **metaphor** is a specific type of analogy. The writer uses a word or phrase to describe something as being another thing which has similar characteristics. For example, the highlighted words and phrases in the following sentence help to create a metaphor for climate change.
>
> *The world **is fighting a battle against** global warming, and it **is a war** that can only be **won** through cooperation between all nations.*
>
> The writer refers to global warming directly in terms of war and fighting. According to this writer, it is not just *like* a war – it *is* a kind of war.

2f Read the following transcript from an academic lecture. The words underlined are metaphors. Work in pairs. Discuss what the metaphorical meaning of the underlined words is. (It is helpful to think of what the word normally means.)

> As the <u>pool</u> of potential students grows, so competition between universities for the best students increases, leading these universities in turn to try to appeal to future students by increasing the range of courses, accommodation and extra-curricular activities available. More choice at every <u>step</u>, more difficulty in making a good choice. This <u>explosion</u> of options can make it very difficult for the student to make a reasonable choice about the most important thing – to stay in education or find a job after school.

2g Read the following sentences from different kinds of academic texts. Identify and underline any words or phrases that seem to be metaphorical. Explain what you think they mean to your partner.

1 One definition of success might be climbing up the corporate ladder, but sometimes those at the top may be neither the best nor the most successful in terms of decision-making.

2 This research has shone much light on the process of decision-making, highlighting the role of intuition and irrationality. However, more research will be needed to illuminate the shadowy area of the role played by emotion.

3 Perhaps the root of understanding of how people make consumer choices is being aware of how perception can grow with experience. This seems to be fertile ground for more research.

4 The foundations of the research appear to be extremely solid, and this has enabled the writers to construct a sound theory of decision-making.

> ➤ LESSON TASK **3 Reading to recognize emphasis in texts**

3a Work in small groups. Discuss these questions.

1 What do you understand by the term 'lifestyle'? Briefly list what aspects might be included in it.

2 It is often claimed that people make 'lifestyle choices'. What kind of choices do you think might be part of this? Make a note of some choices you think would be 'lifestyle choices'.

3b Read this introductory text about the concept of lifestyle choices. Check to see if your ideas in 3a were mentioned.

Lifestyle and lifestyle choices – a general introduction

The concept of 'lifestyle' is a relatively recent phenomenon, at least as far as the general public are concerned. It can be defined (Glass, 2002, p.12) as 'the typical actions of individuals on a daily basis to actively create an environment which they feel is specific to them and in which they feel most comfortable'. Everyone, therefore, has their own distinct lifestyle, and some of the things most commonly associated with it include habits (everything an individual does on a regular basis, from what they eat, the fitness regime they pursue, even bad habits such as smoking), career (the career paths and opportunities a person takes), financial status (although this is not the most important aspect of lifestyle, it does help define the manner in which a person can live in other areas) and emotional state (the adoption of a particular lifestyle is largely about creating emotional peace and satisfaction). Leading what an individual might see as a positive, healthy and productive lifestyle requires conscious effort. The concept of lifestyle is therefore largely connected to 'lifestyle choices', defined by Werther (2003, p.34) as the 'conscious positive decisions made by an individual to change elements of their lifestyle in an attempt to improve it in some way (i.e. one that is more personally satisfying)'. According to Glazer et al. (2005), this could include processes such as identifying problems in an area of lifestyle (for example, lack of income, unhealthy eating habits), setting goals to solve the problems both in the short and long term and actually consciously working towards these goals.

3c You have been asked to write an academic essay with the following title.

Critically examine the reasons for the adoption or non-adoption of vegetarianism.

Work in small groups. Discuss these points.

1 What is the difference between being a vegetarian, a vegan and a fruitarian?

2 Tell each other what 'lifestyle choice' you have made with regard to vegetarianism and why.

3 Brainstorm as many ideas as you can on the points in the table on p.153.

Possible reasons for choosing to be vegetarian	Possible reasons for choosing not to be vegetarian

3d Work in groups of three. Your teacher will give you each one source to read. As well as making notes and sharing ideas, you need to critically read and analyze the sources to find out whether the arguments they put forward are academically sound. Then report back to your group. Follow these steps.

1 Read the source(s) you have been given.

2 Underline any phrases or words which suggest that the writer may not be putting forward an academically sound argument.

3 Highlight any arguments which you think are flawed (i.e. are against the person, not the idea; where the evidence is insufficient; where there are logical flaws, etc.)

4 Give the source a grade on this scale:

Source reference: _____

Very poor academic source								Excellent academic source
1	2	3	4	5	6	7	8	9	10

3e Report your findings back to your group. Use examples from the text to back up your comments.

3f As a group, decide which source(s) would be most useful and why.

3g Work in pairs. Read the sources you have not worked on. Identify any of these features.

- Analogies
- Use of metaphorical language
- Places where the writer has clearly emphasized specific information

4 Review and extension

4a Read these extracts from academic essays or lectures. Underline the form of *like* used in each extract (A–D).

A For the prospective student there are also social issues – how far is the university from your home or friends, what entertainments and amenities are available on the campus, and so on. In this regard, many university prospectuses now appear more like holiday brochures, aggressively marketing their bars, clubs, accommodation facilities and opportunities to socialize.

B Today I'd like to think about the relationship between video games, in particular games which require, or encourage, violent actions by the players, and violent behaviour in the real world. Now violent video games are not new …

C Now, if you're like me, then you probably enjoy living in a society where you have plenty of options available to you. Eleven different varieties of coffee in your local coffee shop, and if you don't like plain coffee then you have a whole bunch of alternative toppings to try. Supermarket shelves stacked with, say, ten different versions of each product, to suit any taste or budget.

D If the boss gives you two jobs and tells you to choose which one to do first – gives you some freedom, in other words – then you're likely, according to the research, to be more motivated, and more satisfied. So we associate choice with freedom, with control over our own lives.

4b Now match the words you underlined in the extracts above with these functions.

Function	Extract(s)
1 to show desire	
2 to show enjoyment or pleasure	
3 to show or suggest similarity	
4 to suggest a high degree of probability	

4c Decide which function of *like* (and related forms) is used in these extracts from different kinds of academic-related texts.

a You need to evaluate your active listening skills and identify areas you would like to improve.

b There is plenty of evidence that people like to have more, rather than less, time to make lifestyle decisions.

c People like Carl Marston would have us believe that climate change is not happening.

d Barlow (2009) seriously exaggerates the risks of climate change, choosing only the most extreme evidence to support his views and enthusiastically agreeing with the predictions of climate models which most other climate scientists believe to be unlikely.

e Taking sensible action now, even if we are unsure whether the threat is real, seems like a wise precaution.

f Making decisions in a crisis is something like driving a car.

g This is not as problematic with simple choices, like deciding which socks to buy, for instance, but can be serious when the problem is one of risk rather than consumer choice.

h Though most lecturers would ideally like their students to pay attention to everything they say, the fact is that during your time in higher education you will sometimes find yourself forced to listen in situations which are not ideal.

i However, as the situation becomes more complex, or more dangerous, and a quick decision becomes necessary, the human mind, like the CPU on a computer, can be overloaded by tasks and fail to reach a timely decision about what to do.

j Omer & Alon (1994) assert that most people in fact remain calm and are capable of making rational decisions for their own safety and that thoughtless panic is rare. However, this seems unlikely.

4d Which of the above examples are analogies?

4e Some common metaphors used in academic texts are related to the general areas in the box below. Match these with the words and phrases in the table. Use a dictionary, if necessary.

buildings   computers   light and darkness   vegetation
war and conflict

Common academic metaphor areas	Commonly associated words / phrases
1	*foundation, collapse, (re)build, (re)construct, groundwork, brick by brick*
2	*illuminate, shed light on, shadow, (in the) dark, highlight, elucidate, shine*
3	*reboot, hard drive, software, process, store, erase, files*
4	*united, onslaught, battle, oppose, attack, bombard, win / lose*
5	*roots, grow(th), branch out, tree, stem (from), plant*

4f Use the words and phrases in 4e to complete these sentences. You may need to change the form of the word.

Example

*Our theory was **constructed** over a long period of time and rests upon a firm foundation of research data.* (buildings)

1 As dementia progresses in old age, the information _____ by the brain as memories is gradually _____ until few of them remain. (computers)

2 The _____ of the problem go deeper than we first thought, and largely _____ from the inability of people to make rational decisions. (vegetation)

3 The data we collected _____ a number of issues which had not been seen in detail before – the idea that emotion plays an important role really _____ through. (light and darkness)

4 Despite the initial _____ by researchers like Simon (1956), the whole argument that people can think and make rational decisions under time constraints has completely _____. (buildings)

5 A number of critics have _____ the rational argument, but there is little _____ to the idea that this way of decision-making represents an ideal or model of how it could most effectively be done. (war and conflict)

Investigating

By the end of Part C you will be able to:

- identify common errors in formality levels of academic emails
- understand appropriate features of emails in different situations
- identify formal and informal language in written communication.

1 Identifying common errors in formality levels of academic emails

1a Work in pairs to discuss these questions.

1 What are the differences between studying in school and studying in a higher education institution?

2 How will the differences at higher education level affect the way you learn?

1b Why might you write an email to a member of staff at your higher education institution? Read the possible reasons (a–k) and decide how likely you think they are. Give each one a score: 1 = very likely, 2 = likely, 3 = unlikely, 4 = very unlikely.

- [ ] **a** asking for a tutorial
- [ ] **b** asking for advice about reading material
- [ ] **c** asking when you can have your essay marked / graded
- [ ] **d** not knowing where your classroom / lecture hall is
- [ ] **e** not understanding a homework assignment
- [ ] **f** not understanding one of the lecturers
- [ ] **g** sending your tutor some work to read
- [ ] **h** when you are having difficulty understanding an idea and would like help
- [ ] **i** asking for paperwork or documentation
- [ ] **j** apologizing for something
- [ ] **k** following up on an earlier email
- [ ] **l** asking for a reference

1c Work in small groups. Can you think of any other reasons?

1d Read these six emails from students to their tutors. Identify the purpose (a–1 in 1b) of each email. (The emails continue on p.158.)

> ☑ New Message
>
> **1** Dear Faye
>
> Hi
>
> this is my essy.
>
> today i want to ask some questions.

New Message

2 Dear Sylvie:

i am waiting for you at 3:15-3:45 PM.in interview room 4 and your office. Burt i can not see you in this period of time. I go to the reception as well to ask how can i find you. The staff just told me to wait for you in 10MINS.if you donnot come, left and send you an email...So i doubty we can change a time for our tutorial....thank you.

New Message

3 Dear Alistair,

I am sorry to interrupt you but last week I did not get the application form for changing the postgraduate major.

 i hope you could sent me the form. i will be very grateful. thank you very much.

I look forward to you!

New Message

4 Ok,my teacher. I will go to see you next Tuesday after I finishing my classes.I feel very sorry about missing my lesson.

New Message

5 Dear Mr Andrew,

I am so sorry to disturb your holiday, but I really need your help.

I am applying a work placement position now.. The key meaning of this email is to ask you helping me send a reference. They said the referee must sent a reference as soon as possible, if not, it would affect my application.

I hope you can spare your valuable time to do this for me. Your prompt attention to this would be greatly appreciated.

I'm looking forwarding to receive your earliest reply.

6 Dear Kim,

I have three questions to ask.

First, have you receive my essay which I send yesterday? I want to know that.

Second, I want to know when term finishes.

Thank you

Yours,

Email offers a convenient way for students and tutors to communicate; however, individuals may have different opinions about the appropriate way to write an email. It is useful to consider these points:

1 Levels of formality
2 Spelling
3 Grammar
4 The structure of the message
5 The opening and closing expressions used

1e Work in pairs. Discuss the differences you think there might be between an email written to:

1 a friend

2 a stranger

3 an academic tutor.

1f Work in pairs. Discuss the problems with the emails in 1d. What errors have the students included? Use points 1–5 in the box above to help you.

1g Work in pairs. Choose two of the emails in 1d. Rewrite them so that they are more acceptable. Then give them to another pair.

Rewrite
1st email:
2nd email:

1h Read the emails you have received. Are there any mistakes? Try to correct them.

2 Understanding appropriate features of emails in different situations

2a Identify each of these features in the email below.

- abbreviations
- contractions
- emoticons
- exclamation marks
- use of first names
- use of opening and closing expressions

☑ New Message

Hi

now i need you to give me some information. I'm so sorry to disturb u. If you are available, would you please make an appointment for me. plz plz plz!! I will contact you. Thank you so much and see you soon ☺.

take care

Olive

2b Work in pairs. Check your answers. Then discuss which features of the email in 2a would be inappropriate if it is sent to the following people.

1 A member of staff in your higher education institution (e.g. a librarian, lecturer or administrator) who you don't know

2 A personal tutor or supervisor

3 A lecturer who you do know

2c Read these three emails (each one is an improved version of one of the emails you read in 1d). What is the purpose of each email?

☑ New Message

1 Dear Alistair

I apologize for missing last Monday's tutorial. I had a headache and fever. Would it be possible to see you next Tuesday?

I'm sorry once again for missing your class.

I hope to hear from you soon.

Best wishes

New Message

2 Dear Sylvie

I waited for you from 3.15 to 3.45 pm outside classroom 4 and your office, but I didn't see you. Could we arrange a time to meet next week?

Best regards

New Message

3 Dear Faye

Please find attached my essay.

Today I'd like to ask you some questions about it. Could you look at it briefly before my tutorial?

Best wishes

2d Now compare these emails with the revisions made by other students in 1h.

2e Read the emails in 2c again. Use the emails to complete as much of the table as you can with examples of words and phrases which perform these functions.

Function	Email	Example word(s) or phrase(s)
Introduce the email / the purpose of the email		
Make a request		
Make an apology		
Conclude the email		

2f Work in pairs. Can you think of any other example phrases? Add them to the table in 2e.

2g Complete the summary below of how to write effective emails with a word or phrase.

> ## Writing effective emails
>
> 1 Always begin your email with _____.
>
> 2 Keep your email _____.
>
> 3 Try to write short sentences and short paragraphs.
>
> 4 Be polite. Use phrases such as _____.
>
> 5 Check your spelling and _____.
>
> 6 Always end your email _____.
>
> 7 Read your email before _____.

3 Identifying formal and informal language in written communication

3a Work in pairs. Look at the following list of problems that a student might have (1–10). Discuss whether it would be appropriate or not to send an email to your tutor or other member of academic staff. Put a tick (✓) if you think an email would be appropriate and a cross if not (✗).

	Situation	✓	✗
1	You have been told that your lectures will be in a different building next week, but you have no idea where the building is.		
2	You don't know how to search for information on the library computers.		
3	You are having trouble understanding some of the ideas in one of your courses.		
4	Your lecturer has asked you to use a software package to analyze statistics, but you have never used it before and don't have a copy of the software.		
5	You have to do an individual research project but have never done one before.		
6	One of your lecturers speaks too fast, gives confusing instructions about assignments and is generally unhelpful towards you and the other students.		
7	Your lecturer has told you that you 'need to improve your writing'.		
8	Your accommodation is noisy and distracting. It's very difficult to study well there.		

9	You don't know how to operate a printer in the library.		
10	You are trying to find information on a topic for an essay but you don't know where to start.		

> Once you have decided that an email is necessary, you need to decide the level of formality you should use.

3b Which of the following phrases are formal, neutral or informal? Tick (✓) the appropriate column.

	Example phrase	Formal	Neutral	Informal
1	Dear Mr Smith, / Mrs Smith, / Ms Smith,			
2	Dear Geoff,			
3	Hi Margaret!			
4	I am writing with reference to ...			
5	I'm writing to ...			
6	Just a quick note to ...			
7	I look forward to hearing from you soon.			
8	Look forward to hearing from you soon.			
9	Hope to hear from you soon.			
10	Yours sincerely,			
11	Best wishes / regards, Best,			
12	All the best, Bye, Bye for now,			

When judging the level of formality to use in an email, there are three key factors to consider. First, how well do you know the person? Writing to someone you know well will usually allow you to be more relaxed about the language you use than writing to a stranger. However, the next thing to consider is the nature of your relationship with the person. Even though you may feel you know your boss or lecturer quite well, you might still use a more formal register in an email to them than you would in a message to someone you had only just met in a social context. The final thing to consider is the seriousness of the topic discussed within the email. A serious topic would usually call for a more formal tone than a short and straightforward message.

So, the most formal tone would be reserved for contacting an employer or lecturer you don't know well with a serious query or piece of information. The least formal register would be used for a short message to a close friend or colleague.

3c Choose one of the situations in 3a. Write an email in the space below, using an appropriate level of formality. Try to use some phrases from 3b.

Notes

3d Compare your email with another student who wrote on the same topic. Did you use the same level of formality?

3e Read these three emails sent by a student to his tutor. What is the purpose of each email?

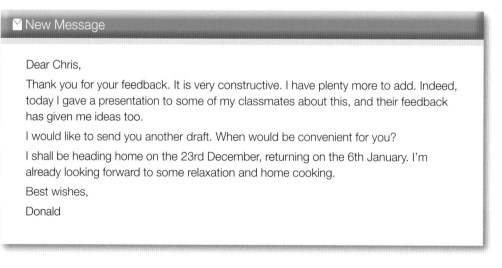

New Message

Dear Chris,

Thank you for your feedback. It is very constructive. I have plenty more to add. Indeed, today I gave a presentation to some of my classmates about this, and their feedback has given me ideas too.

I would like to send you another draft. When would be convenient for you?

I shall be heading home on the 23rd December, returning on the 6th January. I'm already looking forward to some relaxation and home cooking.

Best wishes,

Donald

New Message

Dear Chris,

Following on from our meeting yesterday, I've made the changes you suggested.

Concerning table 5, the numbers refer to the number of options given, which I have now explained in the essay. Does that make sense of the table?

I plan to submit the essay next week.

Hope you are well.

Best wishes,

Donald

New Message

Dear Chris,

This is just to let you know that I've finished going through the options now, and have started planning the essay. Indeed, I'm almost ready to begin writing now, though it's still very rough.

Concerning my essay, I am very keen to look at consumer preferences in detail. I've had trouble finding many sources of information, though. In particular the key text by Kuga isn't in the library. Is it a must to use that book? If it is not a problem, are there any books you would say are vitally important for this topic?

Apart from that, all is well.

Best wishes,

Donald

3f Complete the table below with example language from the emails.

Function	Example features
Introduction	
Personalization	
Informal features	
Question forms	
Concluding remarks	

3g Work in pairs. Discuss how formal or informal the emails are. How do you know?

> **LESSON TASK** **4 Writing a formal email**

4a You are going to write an email to your tutor, Tim Simmonds, telling him about a work placement that you have managed to arrange at a local business. You need to tell him when the placement starts, how long it will run for and what you'll be doing while you're there. You want to get confirmation from your tutor that this placement will be appropriate.

First, briefly note down the details you will need. You will need to invent these.

4b Choose an appropriate opening from the box.

Dear Mr Tim   Good evening   hello, sir   Dear Tim   My tutor

4c How will you open the email? You need to explain why you are contacting them. Write some possible openings.

4d Using your notes from 4a, write the section describing the placement you have arranged. Pay attention to the formality of your language.

4e You need to make sure they understand what response you would like from them. How could you express this in your email?

4f Finally, choose an appropriate sign off from the box.

Best wishes   I look forward to hearing from you   Yours   Thank you

4g Check your email for spelling, grammar and formatting mistakes.

5   Review and extension

5a Read the following essay titles. Identify a difficulty a student might have in answering each question. For instance, there may be phrases in the question that are difficult to understand; it may be unclear where to find information about the topic; or it may be unclear what the task requires.

> **1** *Examine the factors that can affect consumer purchasing decisions. Evaluate the implications of this for the ways companies market their goods.*
>
> **2** *The 'Paradox of choice' has been used to explain why people have difficulty making complex choices and also as an explanation for high levels of stress in modern societies. Suggest an art project or installation that can help people to explore themes of individual choice.*
>
> **3** *What factors do designers and programmers need to take into account in order to make web pages as user friendly as possible? Examine ways that web page designers can ease decision-making by end users.*
>
> **4** *A telecoms company is intending to place a new mobile-phone base station in a residential area, approximately 15 metres from a row of houses. Residents are strongly opposed, believing that mobile-phone towers emit Radio Frequency (RF) energy which is dangerous for health. You have been asked to assess the risk posed by the base station. Evaluate the available information about the potential health risks posed by RF energy from mobile-phone base stations and decide whether it should be moved or not.*

5b Write an email to each of these people in an appropriate style.

- Your lecturer, asking for an academic reference.
- A librarian, asking to reserve a book titled *Sociology* by Anthony Giddens.
- Your personal tutor, asking to arrange a meeting for next Wednesday.
- A telecoms manager, complaining that your last bill was incorrect.

Reporting in speech

By the end of Part D you will be able to:

- conclude an oral presentation
- speculate about research results in conclusions.

1 Concluding an oral presentation

1a Work in pairs. Discuss these questions.

1 What information should a successful speaker include in the conclusion of their presentation?

2 What words or phrases do you typically hear, or would you use, in the conclusion of a presentation? Make a list in the space below.

Notes
In conclusion, ...

1b Work in small groups. Look at the words and phrases you wrote in your answer to question 2 above. What function do you think each one has?

Example

In conclusion, ... – this phrase signals the start of the conclusion

1c Work in pairs. Read the notes below which a student has written while preparing for her presentation. Discuss:

- what you think the topic of her talk is about
- what you think her conclusion is.

Conclusion

Strng rltnshp BTWN 1. cnsmr bhvr AND 2. No. of choices

⟶ SERIOUS implications – for mrkt & retailers

BUT! not all choice shld go – We wnt FREEDOM 2 choose

Evidence: sales rise if choice lmtd

1d Use the student's notes to write expanded notes for a short conclusion on the topic. Make a note of useful phrases you could include to structure your conclusion.

Notes

1e Work in pairs. Take turns presenting your conclusion to your partner. Make a note of the words and phrases they have used from 1a.

▶ 4.13

1f Listen to the student using her notes to conclude her presentation. As you listen, complete the extracts below with one word in each gap.

1 So _____ _____ _____ _____ _____ , *pretty clearly, I think, that …*

2 *I wouldn't* _____ _____ _____ *that all choice …*

3 *… but there is* _____ _____ _____ _____ *that sales can be …*

▶ 4.14

1g Listen to the conclusions to three more presentations (Speakers A, B and C). For each speaker, answer questions 1–5 in the table with a tick (✓) for 'yes' or a cross (✗) for 'no'.

Does the speaker …	Speaker A	Speaker B	Speaker C
1 signal the beginning of the conclusion?			
2 identify and refer to their main argument?			
3 suggest possible implications of their argument?			
4 identify potential future research?			
5 invite questions from the audience?			

1h Listen again. As you listen, try to identify any words or phrases which perform the functions described in questions 1–5 in the table above. Make notes in the table on p.170.

Notes
1
2
3
4
5

1i Read the transcripts in **Appendix 5** and check your ideas. Then identify all the words and phrases which perform the five functions to complete the table below.

Function	Words or phrases used
To signal the beginning of the conclusion	
To identify and refer to their main argument	
To suggest possible implications of their argument	
To identify potential future research	
To invite questions from the audience	

2 Speculating about research results in conclusions

Often, an academic presentation will focus on a piece of (small-scale) research which the speaker has carried out. One function of a conclusion to this kind of presentation may be to speculate about the importance or implications of the results.

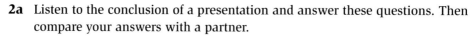

2a Listen to the conclusion of a presentation and answer these questions. Then compare your answers with a partner.

4.15

1 What is the topic of the speaker's presentation?

2 What does the speaker speculate about?

2b Read the transcript in **Appendix 6** and underline any speculative phrases.

2c Work in pairs. Read the transcript of the conclusion of another presentation. The speaker has not used appropriately cautious language to speculate in the conclusion. Use the space provided to rewrite the underlined section of the transcript to include more cautious language.

> So what can we conclude from this? Well, the results I've presented here show that there are some significant differences in the way that students at opposite ends of the achievement spectrum choose to use their non-lecture time. As you've seen from the data, lower-achieving students predictably choose to spend more time on pure leisure activities overall. However, as I've discussed, the results do also unequivocally confirm that all low-achieving students spend an equal amount of time on study as their more successful peers. Causes for this include differences in the approach taken while studying, as well, certainly, as the time when such study is done. However, it is difficult to generalize from the limited sample I have looked at and I strongly urge that further research is needed in order to shed more light on these aspects. I will now happily accept any questions you may have.

Notes

2d Now listen to a different version of the same conclusion, in which the speaker speculates using more cautious language. Make a note of any similarities or differences with your own version. Then check your notes with the transcript in **Appendix 7**.

4.16

2e Match the beginnings with the correct endings of these phrases for speculating on research results.

A	B
1 This is	is needed
2 Further research	be interesting to see
3 shed	that this raises is
4 It would	far from clear
5 It is interesting	the case that
6 It might be	light on
7 An interesting question	to speculate on

2f Work in pairs. Read the transcript of the conclusion to a presentation. Discuss what words or phrases could go in each gap. Some, but not all, of the words or phrases are from 2e.

> 1)_____, we 2)_____ that there are a number of general factors that need to be taken into account when making a decision about how to allocate resources such as money. 3)_____ estimations of the risks and benefits involved in any choice, as well as considerations of the amount of the resource available, and also the priorities with which it might be needed. However, there are a number of external factors, such as bias and time pressure, which 4)_____ this decision. The research evidence which 5)_____ suggests that many people do not make such choices by rationally considering every factor. An interesting question that 6)_____ is whether people who rationally consider all the alternatives actually make *better* decisions than those whose decision-making process is irrational, or intuitive. It 7)_____ that people do not need to consider every possible factor in order to make a good decision about how to allocate the resources available to them. However, the answer to that question is outside 8)_____ presentation. 9)_____ much for listening. Are there 10)_____?

4.17

2g Listen and complete the text with the words and phrases the speaker uses.

> ► **LESSON TASK** ## 3 Presenting results of research

3a Work in small groups. Discuss these questions.

- How many hours' study per week (both in and out of class) do you think students on your course do?
- How many hours per week 'leisure time' do you think students on your course take?
- What kind of leisure activities do you think students on your course do?
- What do you think are the main factors affecting students' decisions about their study / life balance?
- What is your position on students doing part-time work? Why?

3b Work with a partner from another group. Read this information about the task.

You are going to do a small piece of research using other students in your class. The research question you are going to investigate is:

What decisions have students at this institution made about their study / non-study life balance and what factors have influenced these decisions?

You will each orally interview three or four other students using a set of prepared questions, and make a note of the answers you collect. Then you will collate and analyze the results, before presenting your conclusions orally to other students.

3c First work together to prepare some interview questions that will help you collect the data you need to answer your research question. You will probably need at least five or six questions, and each question may have several parts.

Examples

- *How many hours study do you usually do per week? Is this enough? Why / why not?*
- *What kind of activities do you do in this study time?*
- *How long do you study for at a time? Why?*
- *Do you plan your study time using a timetable? Does this work? Why / why not?*
- *Why did you decide to have these times as study time?*

Make sure you leave some space on your question page to note down the answers from your interviews.

3d Interview other students, making brief notes of the answers they give.

3e Work in pairs. Tell each other about what you found out from your interviews. Look at your results and try to draw some generalizations from them.

Examples

- *Roughly, what is the average time spent on study / leisure / part-time jobs?*
- *What kind of study / leisure activities do students do?*
- *What are the most popular?*
- *What reasons do different students give for organizing these times in the way they do?*

3f Prepare the conclusion for a short oral presentation (about three minutes) on the results of your research. Make sure you include the following parts:

- Reference to the research question
- A brief summary of the results
- Some possible implications of the results
- Some limitations of the research
- Some suggestions for further research

3g Take turns to present your conclusion to a different group of students. Answer any questions asked.

4 Review and extension

4a Match the beginnings with the correct endings of these phrases found in conclusions.

A		B
1	In	a strong relationship between ...
2	In	which I've presented here ...
3	I have	very much for listening.
4	There seems to be	summary, ...
5	More research	conclusion, ...
6	The research evidence	any questions?
7	Thank you	would be necessary in order to ...
8	Are there	argued that ...

4b You are going to complete the gaps in the presentation on p.175 about natural resource allocation with the words you hear. Before you listen, read the transcript and try to predict what phrases are used. Do not write your answers on the transcript yet. Make a note of your ideas below (the number of gaps tells you the number of words in each phrase).

Notes	
1	4
2	5
3	6

1)_____ _____ , the world is facing serious resource challenges in the coming years. Supplies of oil and gas, vital minerals, fish stocks, agricultural land, wood, and fresh water, among other things, are finite, and as the examples I have shown **2)**_____ _____ _____ indicate, they are under growing pressure from a combination of rising population, the desire for unlimited economic growth, and existing patterns of overuse. In the coming century, governments, businesses and ordinary citizens will **3)**_____ _____ _____ increasingly difficult choices about how to allocate the resources available to them. Stricter laws will become necessary, and certain items will need to be restricted. However, it is not all **4)**_____ _____: continued increases in the population will force us to develop creative new solutions to the resource problem in order to accommodate everyone. Thank you **5)**_____ _____. Are there **6)**_____ _____?

4.18

4c Now listen and complete the transcript with the words you hear.

4d Read the conclusion to another presentation on the topic of the choices men and women make. Rewrite the underlined parts of the conclusion with more speculative language. Use the space provided.

> In summary, then, <u>it's</u> misleading to talk about a single 'gender gap' when it comes to making career choices. And <u>it's certainly</u> too simplistic to state that this gap is a simple case of men's advantage at women's expense. Instead, it <u>is</u> more correct to view it as a number of different 'gaps', in some cases disproportionately in women's favour, while in others favouring men. An interesting question, which is unfortunately outside the scope of this talk, is what <u>are the effects</u> of these gaps? For instance, the effects of such a large, and growing, number of female university students <u>will lead</u> to changes in subjects offered, studied and <u>even the</u> ways they are assessed. And when it comes to the jobs market, it is <u>certain</u> that the present situation, where women are paid less and often struggle more than men to be promoted at work, <u>will</u> not last much longer. I would suggest that these are areas where more research is needed. Thank you.

Notes

4.19

4e Now listen to the speaker. Make a note of the differences. Then compare the differences with your own ideas in 4d.

Reporting in writing

By the end of Part E you will be able to:
- develop language for writing conclusions
- refer to previous sections of an academic text in the conclusion
- express importance, desirability and necessity.

1 Developing language for writing conclusions

1a Read the conclusions for three different academic research articles (1–3). Then choose the essay title (a or b) which you think is most appropriate to each conclusion.

1

Precise information on the state of resources is vital for effective ecosystem | 1
management. Ecosystems are complex and constantly changing environments and,
though their effective management depends on accurate and reliable decision-making,
their complexity, paradoxically, makes reliable decision-making very difficult. Resource
allocation is a particular issue, and decision makers involved in this process have | 5
previously relied on professional experience alone to help them make resource decisions.
This paper has compared a number of computerized decision-making systems which
can support this process and lead to greater decision reliability. Though both GIS and
DSS decision support software seem to be effective, their combination into an integrated
system helps the decision maker to best allocate resources, where the goal-function of | 10
the software is to optimize resource allocation and reduce wastage. This combination of
software has other applications outside the field of ecosystem management, including
emergency relief and government environmental policy.

a A comparison of software programmes designed for aiding decision-making in ecosystem management.

b Managing ecosystems – the role of computers in improving resource allocation and management decisions.

2

The results presented here suggest that resource allocation decisions made by consumers | 1
are influenced strongly by considerations of value, cost and prestige. Shoppers appear to
allocate financial resources based on intuitive feelings about whether an item is 'positive',
rather than a careful consideration of the benefits involved. Because of the exploratory
nature of this study, we were unable to collect data from multiple respondents, therefore | 5
a number of variables have been derived from only a single respondent. Though the
reliability of these answers from a single source is uncertain, the results provide some
evidence that shopping behaviour follows other types of affect-based decision-making.
The model of shopping behaviour used in our study does not incorporate considerations
of opportunity costs, which is a factor that has a significant impact on the resource | 10
allocation decisions studied here. Further research needs to be done on developing a
more complete model of shoppers' financial resource allocation behaviour. It would also
be beneficial to try to apply approaches from cognitive psychology to understanding
how incentives affect allocation decisions.

a The role of incentive schemes in the financial resource allocation decisions of consumers.

b An investigation of consumers' decision-making behaviours.

3 In conclusion, it is apparent that difficult resource allocation decisions are as   1
common in the provision of medical care as in any other type of field. Resources
such as medical supplies, staff and money for investment or purchase of equipment
are finite, so decisions must be made about how to distribute these for the care
of needy patients. There are obvious ethical dilemmas involved in how to allocate   5
scarce medical resources and, though cost-effectiveness is an unpalatable issue in
medicine, with competition between medical departments for available resources,
many medical authorities argue that it must nevertheless be considered.

   a Factors impacting resource distribution decisions among health professionals.

   b A computer-aided decision-making model for healthcare resource allocation.

1b Identify each of these common functions in the conclusions above. Ignore the right-hand column of the table for now.

Function	Hedging language (Y / N)?
Summary of key points	
Suggesting broader implications of the thesis or findings	
Discussion of implications from key points	
A restatement of the original thesis	
Weaknesses of the research	
Recommendations for further research	

> Conclusions to academic papers often have particular features of language. These include:
>
> 1 direct statements about which the writer is confident, in either the present or past tense
> 2 expressions for emphasis on key points
> 3 hedging expressions which leave room for doubt about claims
> 4 general statements beginning with *there + be / it + be.*

1c Read the conclusions in 1a again and identify examples of each language feature.

1d Check your ideas with a partner.

1e Work in pairs. Complete these activities.

   1 Compare the amount of hedging in the conclusions in 1a.

   2 Compare the differences in the use of hedging in different functions of the conclusion. Complete the table in 1b.

   3 Discuss possible reasons for these differences.

2 Referring to previous sections of an academic text in the conclusion

> The conclusion is an opportunity to summarize the key ideas of an essay or paper; therefore, it plays an important part in making the text cohesive. It is common for a writer to refer to the original thesis statement as well as other key sections mentioned in the main body of the text.

2a In this short extract from a conclusion, underline all the references to the original thesis that the writer makes.

> Concerning hypothesis 1 (see Section 4.1), that decision-making under stress can be improved through training, it seems clear that well-developed training programs can boost this ability, although it is uncertain whether these improvements can be maintained over time without regular retraining.

> When referring to things earlier in the text in the conclusion, these strategies could be used.
>
> **1** Refer explicitly to the idea or thesis.
> **2** Refer to the particular section in the text where it is discussed.
> **3** Summarize in words what it is.

2b Identify examples of these three strategies in the paragraph above.

2c Read the next paragraph. Underline places where the writer refers to previous sections of the paper. Identify which of the strategies 1–3 above the writer uses.

> Regarding hypothesis 2 (see Section 4.2), the results both agree and disagree with the statement that time stress affects the ability to make decisions. For example, more than half of the respondents claimed that they felt greater difficulty in the reduced-time test, which seems to be an indicator of time stress. The results also seem to tally with Berkoff's (2001) ideas concerning timed responses. There was more than the one example of those posited by Mendoza (1975). The quality of decisions made, however, does seem to decline as the time available increases beyond an optimum.

2d Here is another conclusion which refers to a number of different parts of the preceding text. Underline and number the references to these parts of the text. An example has been given to help you.

1 Aims of research

2 Research question / hypothesis

3 Literature review

4 Method

5 Results

6 Discussion of results

The results presented here[5] suggest that resource allocation decisions made by consumers are influenced strongly by considerations of value, cost and prestige. Shoppers appear to allocate financial resources based on intuitive feelings about whether an item is 'positive', rather than a careful consideration of the benefits involved. Because of the exploratory nature of this study, we were unable to collect data from multiple respondents, therefore a number of variables have been derived from only a single respondent. Though the reliability of these answers from a single source is uncertain, the results provide some evidence that shopping behaviour follows other types of affect-based decision-making. The model of shopping behaviour used in our study does not incorporate considerations of opportunity costs, which is a factor that has a significant impact on the resource allocation decisions studied here. Further research needs to be done on developing a more complete model of shoppers' financial resource allocation behaviour. It would also be beneficial to try to apply approaches from cognitive psychology to understanding how incentives affect allocation decisions.

2e Read the following conclusion to a research paper and answer these questions.

1   What were the researchers' hypotheses before they conducted the research?

2   What were the findings from the study?

3   Did the researchers discover anything unexpected?

This study has been extremely limited, due to the limited number of participants. However, it suggests that having an excessive number of choices may reduce the individual's motivation to reach any decision at all. This gives some empirical support to what has been referred to as the 'Tyranny of Choice' (Schwartz, 2000). It also seems likely that restriction of choices can help to improve mood and motivation, and reduce feelings of regret.

In accord with our first hypothesis, that consumers choose more freely when a limited number of options is available, it seems clear that there is a definite preference for a more limited number of options (around six). This conforms to similar findings by Iyengar and Lepper (2000) and others. However, although we expected that respondents would report greater pleasure when faced with fewer choices, we found that this is not always the case. Individuals with high 'satisficing' scores reported approximately the same feelings of pleasure regardless of the number of options, while those with high 'maximizing' scores, surprisingly, showed only a slight preference for reduced options. This suggests that individuals may initially prefer the appearance of greater choice, without being consciously aware that it increases the difficulty and stress of making a decision.

Regarding our second hypothesis, the results support the statement that people faced with a larger range of choice experience feelings of regret more frequently after the choice has been made. Furthermore, they tend to report stronger feelings of regret in these contexts than when presented with a limited number of options. The results also seem to accord with Gilovich and Medvec (1995) and Iyengar and Lepper (2000). Having a very large number of options, then, does seem to present individuals with greater difficulty in arriving at a decision, and also results in stronger feelings of regret after the choice has been made.

2f Now read the conclusion in 2e again and identify the tenses used for the underlined verbs.

2g Use the preceding examples to decide which tense (or tenses) are generally used for these functions.

Function	Tense(s) generally used
Describing the study / research as a whole	
Referring to other researchers' results in general	
Generalizing from your own results	
Linking results to the research question / hypothesis	
Referring to specific findings in your own results	

2h Complete this conclusion with a suitable tense of the verb in brackets.

This study **1)** _____ (give) some support to the claim that having too many choices **2)** _____ (prevent) individuals from making a decision. In our first hypothesis (see Section 3.2), we **3)** _____ (expect) that students would choose to undertake voluntary activities if given a limited range of options. As predicted, the respondents **4)** _____ (choose) more frequently when given a limited number of options than they did when given a wider range to choose from.

We can conclude that both self-identified maximizers and satisficers **5)**_____ (behave) in the same way, and **6)** _____ (make) similar numbers of options in either the limited-option or wide-range conditions, suggesting that decision-making styles **7)** _____ (be) not as influential in behaviour as the number of options presented.

3 Expressing importance, desirability and necessity

3a Read this extract from a conclusion. According to the writer, what further action is necessary, and what further action is desirable?

Further research <u>needs to be done on developing</u> a more complete model of shoppers' financial resource allocation behaviour. <u>It would also be beneficial to try</u> to apply approaches from cognitive psychology to understanding how incentives affect allocation decisions.

Conclusions frequently make strong claims about the importance of their findings. These can be supported by expressions of the necessity of future research or other actions, or less assertive recommendations about desirable actions. This can be expressed in a number of ways, including:

1 Adjectives of necessity or importance
2 Modal verbs showing obligation
3 *There is* + noun phrase
4 Indirect recommendations

> **Examples**
> 1 further research is **vital**
> 2 further research **must** be carried out
> 3 **there is a need for** further research
> 4 further research **would** help to establish this link
>   **it is recommended that** further research be undertaken

3b Some modal expressions of necessity are uncommon in formal written English. Work in pairs. Decide which of these expressions are more appropriate in casual spoken or written English (C) and which are more common in formal written English (F).

1 More research **needs to** be conducted in order to evaluate the effect of choice overload on consumer purchasing decisions.

2 We **ought to** study the effects of choice overload on purchasing decisions more closely.

3 Educators **had better** help their students to improve their ability to make sensible time management choices.

4 International organizations **must** work together with the government to ensure funding for research in order to safeguard our economic prosperity.

5 Researchers **have got to** pay more attention to the relationship between lifestyle choices and environmental impacts.

6 Budget-allocation decisions **should** be based on rational decision-making methods.

3c Underline the key phrases / structures for *importance*, *necessity* and *desirability* in the sentences below.

1 Further applied research is necessary to test the 3-stage Resource Planning model presented here in a real-life resource allocation situation.

2 Further work needs to be done to establish whether a rational approach to consumer behaviour really is more effective in terms of consumer satisfaction.

3 It is recommended that subsequent research be undertaken in the areas of resource allocation and systems management, especially with regard to long-term environmental factors.

4 Further investigation is needed to confirm whether or not this type of software can effectively replace human decision-making in this field.

5 Future research might explore the extent of psychological factors in the choice of university by overseas students.

6 More information on the factors affecting consumer choice would establish if the role of family and friends is indeed as important as these results suggest.

7 We must focus more attention on so-called 'irrational' decision-making processes.

3d Look at some of the grammatical structures you have underlined and focus on the form of the verbs that follow the key phrases. Put the verb forms in this table. Then check your answers with a partner.

	Key phrase	Following verb form
We	need to	
	must	
	is necessary	
	is needed	
Further research	needs to be done	
	might	
	would	

3e Look at this grammatical structure and discuss the questions below.

It is <u>recommended</u> that subsequent research [   ] be undertaken ...

1 What other word(s) could be used to replace *recommended*?

2 What comes after *recommended*?

3 The writer has decided to omit a key part of the structure in [   ]. What word(s) have been omitted?

4 What verb form is *be undertaken*?

3f Use what you have learned to complete this text using a similar pattern, but *alternative* words, to the example above.

It _____ further investigation _____ into the role of economic factors in educational decision-making. It is also _____ further study _____ in the area of educational resource allocation to see if more effective use of scarce resources is possible.

> **LESSON TASK**   **4   Writing a conclusion**

4a Work in groups of three or four. Discuss these questions.

1 Which natural resources does your country produce? Does it export any of these?

2 Which natural resources does your country need to import?

3 What problems might this bring? What are the possible solutions?

4b Read this essay title. Decide on your position for some of its aspects by marking an 'X' on the diagrams below.

To what extent are concerns that finite natural resources (such as fossil fuels, fresh water and agricultural land) are running out justified?

The concerns are   The concerns are not
highly justified.   justified.

|——|

Natural resources   Natural resources
are running out.   are infinite.

|——|

4c Here is a possible thesis statement for the title. Work in small groups. Assume you all agree with this position and brainstorm at least three more supporting arguments and three counter-arguments for it.

> Many natural resources on which the human population relies for survival and economic growth are finite. Continued levels of population pressure and present unrealistic economic growth expectations make it highly likely that these resources will run out, unless decisions are made about how to manage them sustainably on an international basis.

Supporting arguments

1 Many finite resources are being rapidly depleted.

2

3

4

Counter-arguments

1 New oil fields are being discovered every year.

2

3

4

4d Work in pairs. Write a one-paragraph conclusion for an essay based on the title in 4b, to include these parts (in any appropriate order):

- Restatement of the position / thesis
- A summary of the main points of the argument / counter-arguments
- A brief discussion of some of the implications of your argument(s)
- Some suggestions for areas of further research in this topic area.

Notes

4e Give your conclusion to another pair. Read each other's conclusions and identify any typical features of a conclusion that the writer has used.

4f Discuss the extent to which you agree with the conclusions given by the other students.

5 Review and extension

5a Put these sentences from a conclusion in the correct order. Then decide which function each sentence serves.

Sentence	Order	Function
Further applied research is necessary to test the 3-stage Resource Planning model presented here in a real-life resource allocation situation.		
While these problems are undoubtedly significant, they can nevertheless be overcome through planning, preparation and coordination of government with industry and local communities.		
The model potentially offers an invaluable tool for government and business decision makers faced with the problem of how to handle increasingly scarce resources.		
The evidence presented above suggests that we are faced with serious questions about the best way to manage our natural resources in the coming half century.		
Increasing population will put more stress on existing water, food, energy and industrial supplies.		

5b Complete this conclusion with the appropriate tense of the verbs in brackets. Then identify the different functions of each part of the conclusion.

Conclusion	Function
The results **1)** _____ (*present*) here suggest that resource allocation decisions **2)**_____ (*make*) by consumers are influenced strongly by considerations of value, cost and prestige. Shoppers **3)**_____ (*appear*) to allocate financial resources based on intuitive feelings about whether an item is 'positive', rather than a careful consideration of the benefits involved. Because of the exploratory nature of this study, we **4)**_____ (*be*) unable to collect data from multiple respondents, therefore a number of variables **5)**_____ (*derive*) from only a single respondent. Though the reliability of these answers from a single source is uncertain, the results **6)**_____ (*provide*) some evidence that shopping behaviour follows other types of affect-based decision-making. The model of shopping behaviour **7)**_____ (*use*) in our study does not incorporate considerations of opportunity costs, which is a factor that **8)**_____ (*have*) a significant impact on the resource allocation decisions studied here. Further research **9)**_____ (*need*) to be done on developing a more complete model of shoppers' financial resource allocation behaviour. It **10)**_____ (*will*) also be beneficial to try to apply approaches from cognitive psychology to understanding how incentives affect allocation decisions.	

5c Find a journal article or essay in your subject and analyze the conclusion. What typical features can you find?

Appendices

Appendix 1

Now some of these things, like TV and radio, were previously delivered to the home using other devices, but since 2007 there has been an enormous rise in the number of people using the Internet to watch TV shows that they could have watched on their home TV set, or likewise listening to radio shows online rather than switching on a dedicated home radio. The evidence is clear that using the Internet for this kind of content actually requires more power consumption than if the user were to use a regular TV or radio. Looking at the figures for TV, we see here that average power consumption for a desktop computer is between 100 and 150 watts, with a laptop being rather less than half of that. By contrast, TVs stand at 74 watts.

Appendix 2

Text A

The next generation of educational engagement

Diana G. Oblinger

Introduction

While it is commonly accepted that information technology has changed how we work, live, learn, and entertain, we may overlook the impact that IT has had on our learners. Students' attitudes and abilities have been shaped by an IT and media-rich environment. Raised in the presence of video, console, and computer games, students in their twenties may have more years' experience with games than with reading. Has this environment changed student expectations for engagement and fun? Perhaps most importantly, what value can this media form bring to learning environments in higher education?

Today's students are digitally literate. Whether 18 or 48, virtually all learners are accustomed to operating in a digital environment for communication, information-gathering, and analysis. Students also tend to be 'always on.' They are in communication with friends and peers constantly through a mixture of cell phones, instant messaging (IM), and email. Mobility is another characteristic – students are constantly on the move, between classes, at work, or socializing. The current generation of college students (ages 18–22) tend to be experiential learners – they prefer to learn by doing, as opposed to learning by listening. And they are community-oriented. Friends, relationships, and contributing to the community are important.

This article describes the current generation of learners who have been heavily influenced by information technology. It also explores the potential of learning environments that incorporate games and simulations to create greater engagement.

Changes in students

A new generation of students is entering higher education – a group called the 'Millennials' or the Net Generation. NetGen'ers were born in or after 1982 and exhibit different characteristics than siblings who are just a few years older. NetGen'ers tend to:

- gravitate toward group activity
- believe 'it's cool to be smart'
- be fascinated by new technologies
- be racially and ethnically diverse (Howe & Strauss, 2000).

NetGen'ers' learning preferences tend toward teamwork, experiential activities, structure, and the use of technology. Their strengths include multi-tasking, goal orientation, positive attitude, and a collaborative style (Raines, 2002).

Today's 18-year-old college students, born when the PC was introduced, began using computers at an early age. Among this group, 20% began using computers between the ages of five and eight. Virtually all students were using computers by the time they were 16 to 18 years of age (Jones, 2002). Another measure of the ubiquity of technology to today's students is the percentage who own computers. In a recent survey, 84% of college students reported owning their own computer, with 25% owning more than one (Student Monitor, 2002).

Not surprisingly, technology is assumed to be a natural part of the NetGen'ers environment. Virtually all teenagers use the Web for school research (94%), and most believe the Internet helps them with schoolwork (78%). Perhaps most striking is their adoption of the Internet as a communication tool – as comfortable for them as the telephone. Having grown up with both, it may not be surprising. Among teens, the use of instant messaging seems to be a natural communication and socialization mechanism. Seventy per cent use instant messaging to keep in touch. Forty-one per cent indicated they use email and IM to contact teachers or schoolmates about classwork. An even higher percentage uses email to stay in touch with friends and relatives (81%). In fact, a slight majority (56%) prefer the Internet to the telephone (Lenhart, Simon & Graziano, 2001).

By the time students reach age 13–17, they are spending more time with digital media (computer, internet, games) than they are television. Their top internet activities are searching / surfing and communicating, educational activities, followed by games. When students aged 9–17 are asked what they want from the Net, getting new and exciting information ranks #1 (nearly 80%). It is followed within a few percentage points by learning more / learning better. Communication is third (Grunwald, 2003).

The life experiences that shaped today's students are quite different from those of previous eras. Each generation is defined by its life experiences, giving rise to different attitudes, beliefs, and sensitivities. Marc Prensky estimates that by the time an individual reaches 21 years of age, they will have spent:

- 5,000 hours reading
- 10,000 hours playing video games
- 10,000 hours on the cell phone
- 20,000 hours watching TV.

In addition, he estimates the individual will have sent 200,000 emails (Prensky, 2003).

Source: Oblinger, D. (2004). The next generation of educational engagement. *Journal of Interactive Media in Education, 2004* (8). Special Issue on the Educational Semantic Web [www – jime.open.ac. uk/2004/8] Published 21 May 2004

References

Grunwald, P. (September 23, 2003). *Key technology trends: Excerpts from new survey research findings. Exploring the Digital Generation.* Educational Technology, US Department of Education

Howe, N. & Strauss, W. (2000). *Millennials rising.* New York: Vintage Books

Jones, S. (2003). *Let the games begin: Gaming technology and entertainment among college students.* Retrieved July 8, 2003 from http://www.pewInternet.org/reports/toc.asp?Report=93

Lenhart, A., Simon, M. & Graziano, M. (September, 2001). *The Internet and education: Findings of the Pew Internet and American Life Project.* Retrieved October 9, 2001 from http://www.pewInternet.org/reports/toc.asp?Report=39

Prensky, M. (2003). *Digital game-based learning. Exploring the Digital Generation.* Educational Technology, US Department of Education

Raines, C. (2002). *Managing Millennials.* Retrieved January 28, 2003 from http://www.generationsatwork.com/articles/millennials.htm

Text B

Mobile technologies: prospects for their use in learning in informal science settings

Eileen Scanlon, Ann Jones, Jenny Waycott

Introduction

This paper reflects on contemporary perspectives on science learning, together with the experience of a number of projects on mobile learning conducted at the Open University and elsewhere over the past few years, in order to consider possibilities of making productive use of mobile learning in informal science settings. However, there is very little literature, as yet, on the intersection of informal learning, science and mobile learning, so in order to consider the possibilities for this area in the future, we have therefore broadened our scope to include educational projects that are institutionally led (e.g. school projects), the use of mobile devices for leisure purposes (e.g. use in museums or for tourism), fieldwork and the potential for supporting hobbies.

There have recently been significant developments in mobile technologies, resulting in devices that combine telephone and wireless internet connection with some of the functionality of personal computers. Many of these devices are described as handhelds or personal digital assistants (Sharples, 2000). Handhelds have been described as 'flexible tools that can be adapted to suit the needs of a variety of teaching and learning styles' (Curtis et al., 2002, p.30).

Many definitions of mobile learning focus on harnessing such mobile devices for learning, e.g. Traxler (2005) comments that 'Mobile learning can perhaps be defined as "any educational provision where the sole or dominant technologies are handheld or palmtop devices"'. However, as Traxler later points out, such definitions which are based around the technology can be problematic. Our approach to mobile learning, therefore, like Traxler and also in line with Sharples, Taylor and Vavoula (2005), is not to focus on the technology but on the learner being mobile. The important feature of mobile learning is that it is the learner who is on the move.

In this paper, we will consider opportunities for using mobile learning in science settings, particularly for informal learning. As indicated above, given the paucity of literature as yet on very informal uses of mobiles in learning science, we will interpret these terms quite broadly and look across a range of settings in which learning can occur, from formal settings, such as schools or universities, to social structures, such as friendship groups, as well as outlining how hobbies might be supported. First, however, we briefly consider some current perspectives on learning science.

Learning science

Until very recently, work on science learning has been influenced by a focus on the need to help learners develop conceptions of basic science concepts. The dominant perspective has been constructivism. Papers such as Driver et al. (1999) provide good summaries of the recent development in theories of learning applied to science, reflecting a shift from the core commitment of constructivism 'that knowledge is not transmitted directly from one knower to another, but is actively built up by the learner' (p.1). Driver points out that this core commitment is shared by a number of different traditions, e.g. those focusing on personal construction of meanings, those focusing on apprenticeship into scientific practices and those looking at the way that learners are encultured into scientific discourses.

This constructivist perspective in science education, with its different traditions, has been dominant in the work on science education. How this perspective has resulted in implications for instructional practices has also been open to interpretation, but is often linked with the influence of practical experience and inquiry on learning (as in Millar and Linn's comments below):

Science should be taught in whatever way is most likely to engage the active involvement of learners and make them feel willing to take on the serious intellectual work of reconstructing meaning.
(Millar et al., 2001, p.289)

and

Ideally science instruction will ensure that students learn complex science in the context of inquiry and have an experience of mastering new topics or technologies relevant to their personal needs or goals.
(Linn, 2004, p.9)

Contemporary models of science learning depend both on the acquisition and participation metaphor (Sfard, 1998). The acquisition metaphor is associated with traditional views of learning, where knowledge is acquired, whereas the participation metaphor is concerned with more radical social theorizing about the learner. Sfard has noticed the linguistic shift from talking about knowing rather than knowledge or concepts in much recent mathematics and science learning literature. The participation metaphor is useful for our consideration in the area of informal learning in particular, as using this metaphor shifts our ideas about knowledge from something we possess and learning from something to acquire to learning as something we do. She points out the importance of the linguistic shift from talking about knowledge (as something the learner possesses) to knowing (which indicates action), and the consequence for our view of the learner as being interested in participation in certain kinds of activities rather than in accumulating private possessions.

This shift of view about the processes by which learning takes place is accompanied by changes in the way that science educators view what constitutes the components of good science understanding. Rather than simply concentrating on the development of difficult concepts, their scope now is to include the processes of science, and science for citizenship. That is, there is a shift from viewing the key purpose of science learning in schools to be an apprenticeship for future professional life as scientists towards science for citizenship. This will have implications for our view of mobile and informal learning too, in relation to connecting to public accounts of science in museums or new media. The view of science understanding as an integral part of the real-life world of students is also important. One of the consequences of this contemporary perspective on science curriculum and learning is that science educators are looking for ways to demonstrate the relevance of work in classrooms to science learners.

There are also views that the whole process of science learning should be better connected to the world outside the classroom. Sefton-Green argues:

Teachers and other educators just simply need to know more about children's experiences and be confident to interpret and use the learning that goes on outside the classroom – we need a culture that can draw on a wider model of learning than that allowed for at present. Secondly, we need to work within various curriculum locations to develop links with out of school learning experiences on offer
(Sefton-Green, 2004, p.32).

Source: Scanlon, E., Jones, A. & Waycott, J. (2005). Mobile technologies: prospects for their use in learning in informal science settings. *Journal of Interactive Media in Education 2005*(25). Retrieved from jime.open.ac.uk/2005/25

References
Curtis, M., Luchini, K., Bobrowsky, B., Quintana, C. & Soloway, E. (2002). *Handheld use in K-12: a descriptive account*, Proceedings of the IEEE International Workshop on Wireless and Mobile Technologies in Education, Los Alamitos, CA: IEEE Computer Society. doi 10. 1109/WMTE. 2002. 1039217

Driver, R., Leach, J., Asoko, H., & Scott, P. (1999). Constructivism in science education. *Educational Researcher, 23* (7), 5–12

Linn, M. (2004). Using ICT to teach and learn science. In Holliman, R. & Scanlon, E. (Eds.) *Mediating science learning through information and communications technology* (pp.9–26). London: Routledge Falmer

Millar, R., Leach, J. & Osborne, J. (2001). *Improving science education: the contribution of research*. Milton Keynes: Open University Press

Sefton-Green, J. (2004). *Literature review in informal learning with technology outside school: A report for NESTA Futurelab (no. 7)*. Retrieved from http://www.nestafuturelab.org/research/reviews/07_01.htm

Sfard, A. (1998). On two metaphors for learning and the dangers of choosing just one. *Educational Researcher, 24* (7), 5–12

Sharples, M. (2000). The design of personal mobile technologies for lifelong learning. *Computers and Education, 34*, 177–193

Sharples, M., Taylor, J. & Vavoula, G. (2005). *Towards a theory of mobile learning*. Proceedings of mLearn 2005 Conference, Cape Town

Traxler, J. (2005). *Mobile learning: It's here, but what is it?* Retrieved from http://www2.warwick.ac.uk/services/cap/resources/interactions/archive/issue25/traxler/

Appendix 3

Now, as I mentioned at the beginning of the talk, I'd like to explore in some detail the ESA's activities in Earth Observation. But before I move on to that, I'd like to talk just a little bit about the ESA's funding. This next slide ... as you can see ... this next slide gives a breakdown of how the overall budget for the ESA was divided up among its various programmes in one year. Now, as you can see, this chart is quite detailed, so I'm just going to talk you through a couple of key points. Now, not shown here is the total budget for the ESA in 2011, which was in fact a little under four billion euros. Now, admittedly, that sounds like a huge amount, but to give it some context, the UK government spent the equivalent of 140 billion euros on healthcare in the same year, to give one example. Anyway, back to the chart. The ESA's funding is divided into two areas: mandatory and optional. An example of a mandatory programme would be Technology ... here ... and other activities such as developing better information systems, um, training, training programmes and so on. Earth Observation is actually considered to be one of the optional programmes. However, I'd just like to draw your attention to the fact that ... as you see here ... Earth Observation accounted for just over 21 % of the total budget. Now, the reason for this is that certain programmes are only of interest to some member states involved, but not all of them, as we're going to see in this next slide ...

Appendix 4

Armitage, R. (2002). To CCTV or not to CCTV? A review of current research into the effectiveness of CCTV systems in reducing crime. London: NACRO.

Problems

1. Evaluation of effectiveness is not sufficient - Needs more study (p.3)
   Many studies are "methodologically weak" (p.4)

2. Street lighting may be more effective than CCTV.
   (one study = 20% crime ↓ from lighting!!)(p.5)

3. May be a "life-cycle" - i.e. CCTV is effective at first but people soon ignore it.(p3)

4. Invades privacy? - May conflict with 1998 Human Rights Act if it is not managed properly (p.3)

Welsh, B., and Farrington, D. (2007). Closed-Circuit Television Surveillance. In Welsh, B., and Farrington, D. (Eds.), Preventing Crime: What works for children, offenders, victims and places (pp. 193-208). NY: Springer Science + Business Media.

Problems

"Much debate" about effectiveness of CCTV. (p.195)
Many studies of benefit are not conclusive

Evaluates findings from 22 studies.
  1) City centre + public housing → "Mixed results"
                                        (p.198)
  2) public transport "Conflicting evidence" (p.202)
  3) Car parks - Most positive effects.
Overall vehicle crime ↓ 28%!
         violent crime ↓ 3%.
  Effect is "small but significant" (p.203.
However, positive effects) may not continue long after
  first installation (p.206)

Appendix 5

Speaker A: So, to conclude. Following the claim by Schwartz that an increase in the number of choices available makes it more difficult to make any sort of choice at all, I would argue that potential students and their families are faced with such a range of options that it is almost impossible to arrive at a satisfactory conclusion about what to do after graduating from school. I am not suggesting that we should restrict the options of courses, locations or even entertainments available. However, I would conclude by arguing for the need for more and better counselling services to help students handle the range of options available to them as they make this most difficult of decisions.

Speaker B: In conclusion, there are many factors which people must take into account when making decisions about how to allocate limited resources, such as money. However, as I've shown, most people appear to be far from being completely 'rational' – the decisions they make are often clouded by emotional and subjective issues. Also, of course, they don't always consider every factor, and even if they do, they might not think about each factor carefully enough. Well, thank you for listening. Are there any questions, anyone?

Speaker C: So, in summary, I would argue that, despite the lack of really conclusive evidence, there is certainly enough to suggest that there is a link between online games and violent behaviour in real life. What is needed now is more research into the neurological effects of these games, especially on specific areas of the brain associated with moral decision-making. This could be supported by studies of those convicted of violence and would help us establish this link with more certainty. Now, if there are any questions, we'd be happy to answer them now.

Appendix 6

In conclusion, the results of our study appear to show that, contrary to the complaints of parents and teachers, most students are capable of making adequate decisions by themselves about the best way to divide their time between study and leisure. We would suggest, however, that more time and energy is given towards making the study time itself more efficient, since many students claimed that some study tasks were taking far too long. It's also important to note that our study is based on only a very small number of questionnaires given to students on this course, so it would be interesting to see if the same results could be obtained in a wider study involving more students. There is also the question of part-time work, which we didn't consider here as it's neither study, nor leisure. With increasing financial pressure on students, future decisions are more likely to involve this as a crucial factor in the time management of student life, and this might prove a rich area for future research.

Appendix 7

So what can we conclude from this? Well, the results I've presented here suggest that there are some significant differences in the way that students at opposite ends of the achievement spectrum choose to use their non-lecture time. As you've seen from the data, lower-achieving students predictably choose to spend more time on pure leisure activities overall. However, as I've also discussed, the results do also indicate that a large number of low-achieving students spend an equal amount of time on study as their more successful peers. Possible reasons for this include differences in the approach taken while studying, as well, perhaps, as the time when such study is done. However, it would be difficult to generalize from the limited sample I have looked at and I would suggest that further research is needed in order to shed more light on these aspects. I will now happily accept any questions you may have.